The Miracle of
Colour Healing

A fascinating story about a truly remarkable woman ... could
not be more highly recommended.

— *Psychic News*

D1140199

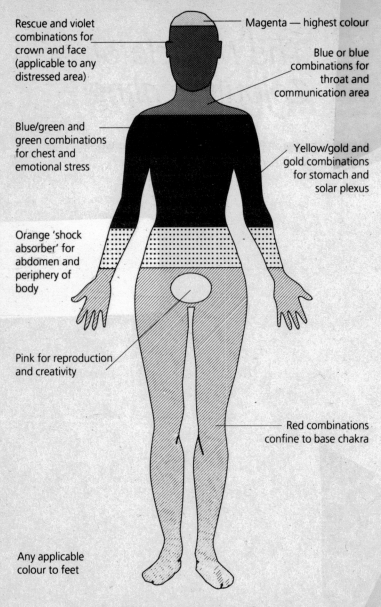

Rescue and violet combinations for crown and face (applicable to any distressed area)

Magenta — highest colour

Blue or blue combinations for throat and communication area

Blue/green and green combinations for chest and emotional stress

Yellow/gold and gold combinations for stomach and solar plexus

Orange 'shock absorber' for abdomen and periphery of body

Pink for reproduction and creativity

Red combinations confine to base chakra

Any applicable colour to feet

Where possible apply around the body to include spine

Aura-Soma chakra chart

The Miracle of Colour Healing

Aura-Soma Therapy as the Mirror of the Soul

Vicky Wall

Thorsons
An Imprint of HarperCollins*Publishers*

Thorsons
An Imprint of HarperCollins*Publishers*
77–85 Fulham Palace Road,
Hammersmith, London W6 8JB
1160 Battery Street,
San Francisco, California 94111–1213

First published by The Aquarian Press 1990
New edition 1993
Published by Thorsons 1995
7 9 10 8

© the estate of Vicky Wall 1991

A catalogue record for this book
is available from the British Library

ISBN 1 85538 289 X

Typeset by Harper Phototypesetters Limited,
Northampton, England
Printed in Great Britain by
Caledonian International Book Manufacturing Ltd, Glasgow

All rights reserved. No part of this publication may be
reproduced, stored in a retrieval system, or transmitted,
in any form or by any means, electronic, mechanical,
photocopying, recording or otherwise, without the prior
permission of the publishers.

Foreword

So many hearts have been touched by this book. The author's sincerity shines through, revealing her as remarkable and God-centred. Those of us who had the privilege of knowing Vicky Wall realized just how generously she gave herself in developing Aura-Soma. The inspired beginning seven years ago and the amazing growth to the present international standing has been the direct result of her reliance on God's guidance. With true humility she always obeyed in faith.

To overcome her severe physical disabilities she had to live a rigorously disciplined life but never did she lose her glorious sense of humour or her ability to love deeply.

Suddenly in January of this year Vicky was called Home to the Greater Garden. Her physical presence is so sadly missed by those who loved her, but we have the consolation of feeling her nearness as we tend Aura-Soma and watch it expand and flourish, always relying on Divine wisdom to guide and direct us, and Divine healing to flow through our fingers.

Since this book was first published Vicky lectured in many European countries including Germany, Switzerland and France. Now we must complete her vision and lecture in Holland and Spain and then overseas in the Americas and South Africa. There is already a second generation of Aura-Soma therapists in Queensland, Australia, where two of Vicky's therapists have taught and trained. Now the other Australian states are asking for lecturers and so the light shines on.

As this book is read may it touch many more hearts and bring many more members into Vicky's Aura-Soma family, that her vision for this 'Re-new-all' age may be realized through each of us.

Margaret Cockbain
Dev Aura, Tetford, 1991

This book is dedicated to my beloved father, with whom all things were possible; to Ann Whithear, scribe and friend, without whose sensitivity and understanding this book would not have been written; to the many others who worked in the background to buy me time to write; and last but not least, to my very dear friend Laura Fraser who shared my dreams and sustained me when in doubt.

Contents

Introduction

Tread softly my friends, for you tread upon the fabric of my life,
the warp and the weft of it, the pattern woven from the beginning
of time, the repeat performance, the inevitabilities pre-ordained,
the progress towards a purpose waiting to be revealed.

I was born in London, a seventh child of a seventh child. My
father and his parents belonged to the Hassidim, a deeply
religious sect involved in the mystical aspects of the Bible. My
father was a master of the Kabbalah and the Zohar and from
his background he inherited a knowledge of the medicinal and
healing qualities of living plants and natural methods of healing
which he passed on to me. The happiness I shared with my
father was, however, badly marred by the secret cruelty of a
vindictive stepmother which resulted in my leaving home at the
early age of 16.

Recurring mystical experiences throughout my childhood,
unsought and frightening at the time because I did not understand them, involved spontaneous healings, realization of auric
sight and clairvoyance, which continued during the intervening
years that led to wartime.

Wartime itself, with its affinity to injury and death, clearly
showed a pattern to my auric sight, a spiritual survey. But
the most eventful meeting that was to set me on my pre-
ordained path was in West Drayton, Middlesex, with Edward
Horsley M.P.S., an elderly pharmacist who was still practising
the arts of the apothecary where herbs hung and pill masses
were handmade and dispensed at the pharmacy. Here, safely
in the labyrinth of learning, I could rediscover and express the
teaching of my father. Within this period many little miracles

of alchemy made their appearance. Once a shortage of ingredients and a mistake led, through inspiration, to a completely new formula which became a remarkable healing agent.

After the war and Mr Horsley's demise I decided to train as a chiropodist where my hands could be used as a healing extension. My first practice was at the pharmacy. Then a Divine Nudge took me to Great Missenden in Buckinghamshire. It was during my years there that I suffered three near-death experiences from which I believe I was saved to serve.

Another disaster, my sudden loss of sight, removed me effectively from a now prosperous Clinic and thrust me out and into an early retirement. But my road to Damascus brought me to a blinding revelation, the birth of Aura-Soma 'Balance' oils that were to heal and change the lives of so many and prove a mirror for the soul.

A unique facet of colour therapy was thus evolved embracing many live energies. A therapy that heals on all levels, physical, mental and spiritual and lends itself as an adjunct to many other therapies.

I now find that more and more of my time is spent lecturing internationally. It became obvious we needed a centre where therapists and laymen would be trained as well as teachers to go out world-wide. Miraculously, Dev Aura in Lincolnshire became our centre and students now come from all parts of the world eager to be pioneers with this New Age therapy.

It is noteworthy, I think, that the first New Age promise was given to Noah when the earth and its people were in danger of being destroyed by human folly. Today, many hearts tremble with fear under the threat of who may push the button and when. Nevertheless there was a promise of a new life with the coming of Christ who spoke repeatedly of a Second Coming and a New Age. Many wait for this but I sincerely believe it is already here. The significance in the promise given to Noah is that never again will God allow the world to be destroyed. His covenant was depicted for the first time through the full spectrum of colour in the formation of a rainbow –

*I do set my bow in the cloud and it shall be for a token of a
covenant between me and the earth.*

Gen. 9:13

Each day with Aura-Soma a fresh aspect appears. It is an ever-
growing therapy. This introduction is but a casting on of
stitches.

O My Beloved Father

When my mother fell ill with 'Spanish' 'flu' in 1918 my father tried desperately to save her. He tried hydrotherapy, wrapping her in a wet blanket and lying beside her in a vain attempt to break the fever. But war and many children had taken their toll. When she died, father's heart was buried with her. Thankfully, when my eldest sister also contracted the influenza she survived.

Father was now left with the responsibility of caring for me (a practically new-born infant) plus six other children climbing up the steps of time at intervals of two or three years. In such a situation there were only two courses open to him – to employ a housekeeper or to remarry. He chose the latter.

My stepmother, of Polish origin, was short and ample in proportions. She had expressive blue-grey eyes that could change in an instant from softness to a look of absolute cruelty, like a cat's contemplating a suffering mouse. This look was to burn itself into my very being, haunting my dreams for many years. She loved her husband and longed to bear his child, but she was barren.

Being only a few months old, dependent entirely upon her, I believe I became, in her mind, the child she had wanted to conceive. Apparently, even at that tender age, I bore a vague resemblance to my father, not my mother, thus helping her illusion. My memory penetrates back to my early babyhood, and even to the pre-birth period, which is one of the unusual faculties I possess. I have no recollection of any disharmony or trauma for the first two or three years, when I feel I was treated and regarded as her natural child. I alone of the seven children called her 'Mummy'. My brothers and sisters addressed her as

'Aunt'. However, they resented her presence, since she had been brought into their lives just a few short months after the loss of their own mother who had truly loved them. Thus the relationship between the older children and their stepmother grew strained.

My father was kept in complete ignorance of the situation, out of their loyalty and love for him and in order not to disrupt his life. My stepmother was an excellent cook, the most competent of housekeepers, and saw her husband's needs as paramount. Under her iron rule, the house ran like clockwork – she had a fixation about the home and possessions. But it was no place for a child – books, toys and playmates were never allowed to invade the spotless home. She was fanatical in this, so it was not surprising that my brothers and sisters and I found we could not relate to her. One by one the older children went their individual ways, leaving me without companionship in the unloving atmosphere of that pristine palace.

My brothers and sisters saw our father regularly, and they would return home occasionally. On one of these short stays something happened that would cloud the rest of my childhood. Sadly and ironically, it was the sister who most loved me and had come to visit me who triggered off the ill-fated sequence of events. Chatting to her, prattling on as a child is wont, I must have sprinkled my sentences with 'Mummy said' and 'Mummy did', for at that time my stepmother was a true mother figure to me.

Imagine my childish interest when I received this sudden information from my sister: 'She is not your mother, and you don't have to do everything she says!'

The moment passed, but the news had been absorbed. Later that day my stepmother and I found ourselves at odds over some minor matters, a little tussle so well known to all parents with wilful offspring. I cannot remember what it was about, but it obviously entailed my co-operation. We had reached the point of no return. I felt threatened, cornered. A recent memory stirred. Looking up at her defiantly, I said: 'You're not my mother. I don't have to do anything you tell me.'

There was a long silence. The blue-grey eyes turned to steel and in that moment the gates of hell clanged behind me. From then on everything changed. Her self-deception shattered, I became the whipping boy for all her frustrations and resentments. The following years bring to mind the words of Elizabeth Barrett Browning: 'For tears have washed the colours from my life.'

I have no doubt that my stepmother, with her cruelty, fulfilled a purpose, and that it was a learning period for me. Now, looking back, I touch the real essence of her actions and understanding brings forgiveness.

As a small child, cut off from companions, I cried secretly into my pillow each night. My sole consolation was the knowledge that my dear father would return home soon. He never failed to come and bid me 'Goodnight'. My bedroom was next to the dining-room, and, perhaps out of habit from babyhood, doors were never shut, so that both my bedroom door and the dining-room door would be ajar. The knowledge of my father's presence in the house, the comforting sound of his step, seemed to bring healing for all the unhappiness I felt caused by the misunderstandings and misfortunes that had befallen me during the day.

I would lie there entranced. I could observe the table, with its napery gleaming white and the silver shining. The candle-light would glow warmly through the carafe of wine. Each evening the same ritual was observed. My father and stepmother would begin the evening meal at seven o'clock and discuss the day's events. Eagerly I would watch the movements of my father's hands as he prepared the pear he always had for dessert. I knew that the precious moment would shortly arrive when he would enter my bedroom and present me (my tears long since dried) with the last succulent sliver of pear, before kissing me 'Goodnight'.

In the early part of this century, children were seen and not heard, and the saying 'Early to bed and early to rise' was widely put into practice. Our household was no exception. My father's homecoming each evening meant much advance preparation. So, in winter, I was usually confined to my bedroom by four o'clock.

The hours between four and seven o'clock were waiting hours of expectancy, and nothing would have induced sleep until my father's appearance and his bidding me 'Goodnight'.

As I lay there in the dusk before the lamplighter came to light the gas lamp directly outside my bedroom window, strange visions would float into my consciousness. This sensation occurred at regular intervals during my childhood and has continued throughout my life. I would find myself singing softly strange cadences and even stranger words, whose meaning and sound seemed to have no real link to the world about me. Yet, mysteriously, it was as if I were using a language of long ago and to which I could relate naturally.

One particular vision kept recurring. Suddenly the room would become diffused with light and I would be aware of a tall, gaunt woman, painfully thin, beside whom walked an equally emaciated hound, its ribs showing starkly; the evidence of starvation was clearly written on both faces. But there was an air of breeding and dignity about them; their nobility shone through. Even as a small child of three years, I felt no fear, no apprehension, as night after night they came, passed through and on. Although I bemoaned their state, something within me knew that this was a situation they had chosen. It was a path they had meant to tread. This vision recurred for many years until one day, in yet another vision, the explanation was revealed. From that time on they went to their eternal rest, only to return in their real role in this life, thus enabling me to understand the full impact of what I had been experiencing.

This was my first acquaintance with 'regression' – an awareness of the past relating to the present.

Father's province appeared to be healing just as my stepmother's occupation, and preoccupation, was with the house. I have no recollection of a doctor ever being called to the house. From early childhood father saw to our every need and tended our various ailments. I was very prone to tonsillitis.

At one time I had quinsy and would cry miserably with pain. To this day the acrid smell of hot vinegar brings vividly to mind the sight of my father painstakingly folding brown paper, pouring vinegar between the folds, wrapping the whole in a linen handkerchief and placing a hot iron over it all. The handkerchief would then be tied carefully around my throat, and in the morning the pain would have subsided. Years later I found the explanation for the success of the treatment, which had its roots in ancient lore. The Kraft paper that was used back in those days was milled from wood pulp. One could actually see the wood fibres in the paper. The therapeutic essences and resins – the basis for many balsams – were fully retained. These would have been dissolved in an alcohol or acid, and heat would then have released them.

All week I would long for the weekend, the precious time when my beloved father would take me on various expeditions. Men in that era were very much given to a strict routine and he was no exception. I knew exactly where we would be going and what the day entailed.

The first call on a Saturday morning was certain to be to the barbers – in those days men shaved, and were shaven, with a cutthroat razor. Father was a handsome man with beautifully expressive, warm brown eyes that seemed to transfix the person he was conversing with. It had been said of him that when he looked at one it was as if two candles would light in the altars of his eyes. His hands were not large but beautifully shaped with 'filbert' nails. He was broad-shouldered, slim-hipped and upright. I have been told that he never put on an ounce of flesh to the day he passed away at 85 years of age. There was about his bearing something truly regal, but he was nevertheless a humble, gentle man. I never heard him raise his voice; a straight look sufficed. He dressed immaculately. He was fastidious and spotlessly clean in everything – a man who held his temple in respect. We children loved and respected him utterly.

At the barbers father would have a shave, hot towels and very often a trim. I would sit patiently on the little wooden bench, completely absorbed by the performance, holding my breath when the hot towels enveloped his face until only the pink tip of his nose was left to view. I always worried that he would not be able to breathe, and was immensely relieved when the towels were unwound to reveal his dear face unharmed. Then what looked like a small block of ice was rubbed on his face. Now I know it was alum, which helped to close the pores and tighten the skin. Alum is used in many astringent lotions today.

Next we would go to father's club where I would be ensconced on a high stool, and given into the care of what I presume was a porter or attendant. A bar of chocolate would be purchased – a great once-a-week treat. Father would place his large white handkerchief around my neck so that I would not mark my dress. Then he would disappear into the inner sanctum of the club, where women and children were never allowed. My child's mind imagined him taking part in all sorts of fascinating happenings. One day, however, my brother, who had been permitted to enter the sanctuary, informed me that there they played chess!

In due course father would emerge and my face would be wiped clean of any trace of chocolate. Now I knew my joy was to commence. We always took the same route past a very high-class fruiterers, where we would stop for purchases. They sold fresh pineapple in long slices from a huge glistening glass jar, and, no doubt mindful of a child's thirst, my father would allow me a slice of this delicious delicacy. I would watch fascinated while the selected slice was removed from the jar with a long two-pronged fork, praying that none of the precious piece would drop off in the manoeuvre. This had happened once and Daddy, a stickler for good manners, had insisted I accept the remainder without murmur.

I would stand and consume the dripping pineapple with great relish. Meanwhile, father would choose certain fruits from the shop, picking them out very carefully for himself. I never saw any exchange of money, and at that age, five or six years old, the world of accounts was unknown to me. I would gaze admiringly at my father and think of him as God, for it seemed that he could take whatever he wanted. When father read to me from the Bible, 'All the fruits of the earth are His', I truly believed that this was proof positive.

And so to Victoria Park – a huge park in London, north of the Thames. Father's work obviously decreed that we should live in this vicinity and I loved it.

This park held many fascinations for a small child interested in everything that moved or breathed. Tame deer would approach, seeking tit-bits. Daddy always brought a good supply of food scraps cut into neat little chunks and carried in a white linen bag – no paper bags for him. He appeared to know each deer by name, and they seemed quite unafraid of him. We would walk on, saying a solemn 'Good Morning' to the parrots in the parrot house. I was rather frightened of them, with their hooked beaks and raucous voices.

As we neared the pond, I would stop to watch the barefoot children, their boots flung round their necks, wading in the water holding little jam jars and home-made nets, trying to capture the rainbow-coloured sticklebacks. I was never allowed the luxury, as I saw it, of joining them. Father was well aware of the dangers of bare feet on broken glass and, more than once, had helped tend an injured child. He forbade me ever to enter the pond. I was charmed by the glistening little fish moving in the jar of water, but I was saddened once when I noted one or two of them, either from shock or mishandling, floating upside down, approaching death. Thereafter I had no real desire to capture them.

Father was absolutely in tune with the animal and plant kingdom, and as we walked he pointed out the many varieties of wild flowers that abounded there. 'Which one', he asked, 'do you think would do poor Daddy's hand good?'

Of course there was no bad hand, but I would trot eagerly around the herbs and flowers, feeling which one would be of help to my beloved father. Thus he taught me to open myself to an instinct within me, an instinct that he obviously had already. I found it exciting when he explained the herbs and flowers to me. There appeared to be a love for them pouring out of him, and he seemed to have an intimate knowledge of their healing properties. I was not allowed to pick even one stem – 'Unless you have a need for it', he said. 'You must never waste a life.'

This was all very real to me, and I remember my great sadness when I watched bluebells being torn from their homes with the sap, their lifeblood, pouring from them, only to find them later strewn on the wayside, bereft, forlorn, left like wasted life on a battlefield.

These days of growing with my father were what my hungry young heart longed for. Through him I was made aware of all living forces of the seen and the unseen. We seemed to be united in an inner knowingness that, as a child, I recognized and accepted without questioning. In the same way, no doubt, my father had been joined to his father; and his father to his father and so on. One had a feeling of a long chain stretching back and back into eternity.

Many strange incidents and healings took place which my child's mind acknowledged without full comprehension. The pattern was repeated throughout my life and eventually realization and understanding dawned.

The Secret

The day had held the promise of happiness and excitement. It was 20 August, my eighth birthday. I dressed quickly but carefully in my school uniform consisting of navy blue knickers with a pocket, black drill gym-slip with belt and a white shirt blouse above it. My whole being was coloured with expectancy.

The morning did not fulfil its promise. Instead, dark clouds of disillusionment and humiliation loomed. Children can be very cruel. My black-robed friends followed me, chanting with derision. Tears of hurt and uncertainty trickled down my cheeks. Suddenly I knew the bitterness of isolation.

It was lunchtime and my father had just arrived home for his meal. Unseeing, I ran full tilt into him as he entered the door. His warm hands held and steadied me. I buried my head in his waist. I felt a magical peace, the turbulence died down, and the sobs subsided.

'What is it?' he asked gently.

Naming two of my particular friends I told him that they had said I was barmy and wouldn't play with me. For a second, I thought I saw a flicker of a smile in his eyes.

'What did you say to them?'

More sobs of humiliation, then: 'All I said was that they had pretty colours around them.'

His eyes contemplated me gravely. 'What colours do you see around me?'

Startled, I told him.

'Hmm,' he said, and now a smile had definitely come into his warm brown eyes. 'Would you like to know what colours Daddy sees around you?'

Suddenly the sun shone and sanity returned. My dear father

had identified with me, and God was in His heaven once more.

'You see,' he explained, 'it's a gift we've both been given. I have it, you have it and your grandfather had it. But the time has not yet come to say so, for the world is not ready. One day, though, you will be able to speak up and they will not call you mad.'

He took my small hand in his and, as was his custom when about to leave me for a while, pressed a kiss into my palm, closing the tiny fingers around it.

'You know what Daddy always says, this is our secret. Nobody knows what you hold in your hand or can take it from you, just like the colours you and I know about. It is our secret.'

As an old soul, he would speak to me as to an understanding equal. 'You are,' he said 'an ancestral echo of an echo of an echo.'

At that time the import was too great for me to grasp, but it was father's way of implanting into my receptive mind that which I would understand later when the time was right. Little did I know that 60 years would elapse before my hand could be opened and my secret gift shared.

The First Healing

Cecilia was my classmate. We were inseparable at school. We sat together, chose each other's company at playtime and walked home together. Most children would invite their friends home to play, or to tea, but I rarely accepted an invitation from anyone as I knew that I could not reciprocate owing to the strict regime of my stepmother. She did not allow playmates in the house for fear of the home being disturbed.

The bell had rung, releasing us for the few precious minutes of hilarious freedom on our way home. Satchels were grabbed, hats smacked on heads and the chatting would begin. Cecilia and I, aged about 11, felt very superior. We, of course, did not engage in idle chatter. Instead, arm in arm, we would saunter off, putting the world and its inhabitants to rights.

Cecilia, born of Irish parents and no doubt named after the patron saint of musicians, was a gentle, dreamy little soul whose lovely blue, black-lashed Irish eyes often held a distant, foreknowing look, completely unrelated to this world. We seemed in perfect tune, both acutely aware of the beautiful things in life. Even at that age, the poetry in our souls was being expressed. But make no error, we were normal, healthy children who were perfectly capable of all the usual youngsters' pranks. I think our backgrounds, although very different, ran along the same disciplinary lines.

As we strolled home together that afternoon, I was startled when Cecilia suddenly stopped abruptly.

'Oh, I almost forgot,' she said. 'I was supposed to call in on my aunt. Mother worries about her so – Aunt's got something wrong and has to stay in bed all the time. Will you come with me? I shan't be long.'

I looked at her, a little alarmed. 'Don't forget, Cecilia, if I don't get home in time for tea there'll be trouble. How long will you be?'

I knew I would be severely reprimanded if I was late – like all meals in our household, teatime was rigid. Cecilia glanced at me sideways. She knew her friend well, and her weaknesses.

'My aunt always gives me a lovely piece of fruit cake when I go,' she murmured slyly.

Now she had indeed touched a vulnerable spot, and knew it. Although our household had plentiful and good food, fruit cake for tea was a rarity. Bread and butter, lettuce and cheese was our usual fare, as sweet things were not greatly encouraged.

'All right,' I said weakly, 'but promise you won't be long.'

From the knob in the centre of the front door dangled a piece of cord, which apparently one had to pull to gain entry, having first announced one's arrival by a call through the letter box. When I think of today with all its hazards, I shudder, but in those days such an arrangement worked simply and safely. Ceremony completed, we entered the bedroom. Spotlessly clean, sparse in fittings, the only furniture apart from one chair and a dressing table was the large double bed, its big brass knobs shining brightly. My bosom pal, with the familiarity of friendship, proceeded to seat herself upon the solitary chair.

'Hello,' I said shyly to the recumbent figure in bed, and stood, for I saw no alternative. The woman, pale, thin and drawn, smiled weakly up at me. Her eyes fixed upon mine.

'Come and sit here, dear,' she said faintly, patting the bed. I had been taught that one should never sit on a sick person's bed, but there was no choice. She reached out to draw me nearer, and somehow did not relinquish my fingers. Cecilia, gazing hungrily at the huge fruit cake sitting in splendour on a plate on the dressing table, asked rather pointedly: 'Would you like some tea, Aunt? Shall I cut you a piece of cake?'

Again the warm smile. 'Thank you, dear, and cut a piece for yourself and your little friend.'

Still she did not release my hand and I found it a little awkward to cope one-handed with the hunk of delicious fruit cake that had been passed to me on a plate. However, love will find a way, and it found its path straight to my mouth, not a crumb dropped. I politely answered all the usual questions: 'What's your name? Are you in Cecilia's class?' Then I started worrying about whether I would be late home. My hand was tingling, a most peculiar sensation, and although I was anxious to depart, it seemed almost as if I would be unable to remove my hand even if I tried. This would occur again and again throughout my life whenever I came into contact with one who needed healing. It was not generally a conscious act and only once was it done by request. At last the tingling ceased and I moved my hand away gently.

'Must go', I said. 'Thank you for the lovely cake.' I almost ran out of the room. Cecilia said her goodbyes and hastened after me.

'Smashing bit of cake, wasn't it?' was her first comment (nothing about her aunt, yet I knew Cecilia loved her aunt).

I was late and, as I had dreaded, was made to suffer for it. I vowed silently never to be caught like that again. Three times after that I was invited to visit Cecilia's aunt, but with the memory of the punishment in my mind, I declined the invitations. The fourth week and Cecilia had me cornered.

'My aunt has been asking why you don't come to see her. She's very upset about it.'

I weakened and I went. The same sequence of events occurred. I held her hand, the tingling started, then I left and the same punishment was meted out for being late home. At the next invitation even the temptation of the excellent cake failed to attract me. The following week, however, Cecilia could not contain herself. She was literally hopping up and down with excitement.

'You must come. I've got something to show you!'

'What is it?'

'A secret', she replied enigmatically. What psychology! I went.

This time there was no string hanging from the door knob. Cecilia knocked and, lo and behold, her aunt stood there, much taller than I had imagined, and much thinner too. But there she stood, smiling broadly.

'Come in, my dear', she said, 'I've been waiting to thank you.'

She embraced me and I felt vaguely disturbed. Thank me for what, and why was she walking? We had tea together, but by now I was fidgeting, shifting from foot to foot, anxious to be off.

'I can see you are in a hurry,' said Cecilia's aunt, 'and I don't want to get you into trouble. Just wanted you to know that you healed me, and I am forever grateful.'

I thought she was quite mad, and couldn't get away quickly enough. Somewhere in my being there was a stirring, a fear of the unknown, a reluctance to think any more about it. After that visit I was adamant, I never went back.

My Cecilia left this world for the angels at the tender age of 13, having lost her battle against tuberculosis. I mourned the passing of my dear friend, but have met her so many times since: it is as if there had been no parting. Before she went, Cecilia told me that her aunt, bedridden for many years, had had a visitation a few months before my visits, informing her that a child would be sent to heal her.

Who Are You?

After the fateful confrontation with my stepmother, things gradually deteriorated. I found myself in the same position as my brothers and sisters, but with a difference. While they had constituted an intrusion on her life with my father, my part had gone much deeper. She had lived in the imagination that she was truly my mother, and the shattering of that illusion had brought forth hate, venom and physical violence.

The pattern continued, becoming unbearable. Eventually, at the age of 16, I left home, taking nothing but the clothes I was wearing.

It was a warm, sunny day with a faint hint of autumn. The trees and foliage around gleamed in the haze. I sat on the park bench, drank in the air and felt the peace that is given when one seeks to identify with nature. I had drifted away into my own thoughts and space. Then, unexpectedly, a voice close beside me said: 'Do you mind if I sit down?'

I found myself looking into the rather haggard face of a woman of around 40. I must confess the intrusion upon my privacy was not exactly welcome. Nevertheless I exchanged the usual pleasantries with her. Suddenly she leaned forward, looked intently at me, and said: 'You're clairvoyant, aren't you?'

Startled and astonished, I stared back at her. Clairvoyant? My father and I knew ourselves only as we were, without the complication of categories. What we gave came naturally, unbidden and unsought. It was the first time I had been faced with the question, 'Who are you? What are you?'

Part of me wished suddenly to move away, feeling threatened. I gathered my thoughts quickly, for the woman was watching me intently, waiting. Then, perhaps sensing that she had been a little too abrupt with her question, for I was very young, she said: 'I only live over the road. Would you care for a cup of tea and a piece of cake, perhaps?'

It seems that the devil's bait has appeared in the guise of fruit cake and tea throughout my life, for on several occasions when a surprising incident occurred fruit cake had been the final drawing power, the penalty of ever hungry youth.

The tea was lovely and hot and the cake fulfilled its promise. Relaxed, I prepared to thank her and depart.

'Help me,' the woman said suddenly. 'You could. I am very unhappy and worried.'

Her words assailed my ears, and in spite of my instinctive recoil, I heard to my astonishment my own voice uttering words I would never have thought to hear: 'That which you are doing is wrong. You are having an affair with a young man who is tied up with your family. It is not right. No good will come from it.'

As the words left my lips I could have wished them withdrawn. What on earth possessed me to say that? Her eyes brimmed over.

'You're right,' she said. 'It's my son's friend. We're having an association. He's living here. My son is unhappy and wants to leave home. I'm torn between the two, but feel unable to break it.'

'It will be broken for you,' I said.

I rose from my chair, making politely for the door. Inwardly, I was very disturbed. As I was crossing the room, the door burst open and a big, burly figure stood there.

'It's him,' she whispered. 'Could you have a word with him?'

The situation had developed rapidly and I was being thrown into a dimension I had never experienced before. There seemed to be a compulsion going beyond the repulsion that I felt. It was as if there was a purpose fulfilling itself in spite of my resistance. I must admit to having been frightened. I prayed silently and started to throw a circle of protection around myself. But it was too late, for I found myself being ushered into the next room and the door closed firmly behind the man – a young man of about 20 – and myself. He leaned towards me, scanning my face anxiously.

'What can you tell me?' he demanded.

Oh, I would have had done with it all. But again, I heard once more a voice that did not even seem to sound like my own saying: 'You are involved in bad things. It is not good.'

'What things?' he asked.

'Money.'

'Money! What money?'

'Bad money,' I responded. 'A lot of money.' The figure of £500 flashed into my mind. I stated it. He made no comment. The voice beyond the voice continued: 'You will have it, but you will not have it.'

The inanity of the utterance struck me immediately. You have it, you do not have it. What nonsense! I felt it would be wise to make a rapid retreat.

'Can you tell me any more?' he asked, pale now and with a desperate note in his voice.

'No,' I replied firmly, though feeling far from firm. 'I really must go.'

Reluctantly he opened the door for me and I left without further delay. The atmosphere within the flat had held a frightening quality, for I had felt through my inner awareness the disharmony and evil vibrations there. Hurriedly I returned to the park, where I gulped in the fresh air and waited for sanity and security to be restored.

This was the first of many such experiences I was to have as I matured. Always unsought, I received on occasion not only glimpses of the future but also glimpses of the past. These reoccurred again and again in everyday meetings and were everincreasing. I did not speak about them. I felt it was not an area in which I had to dwell continually, but that this particular faculty should be used only to help when it had a purpose. Never have I used it as an entertainment.

A week or two later, scanning the local newspaper, I read that the park pavilion had been broken into and stocks of cigarettes stolen. (The robbery had taken place about two days before my encounter with the woman and her boyfriend.) The report went on to tell that a man had been caught selling the cigarettes to a receiver, that £500 had been recovered and that the man had been sentenced to six months' imprisonment.

Thus was the association effectively broken, as foretold.

The Apothecary

The war had been with us for one year and I was now living in
West Drayton, Middlesex. My way home from the station led
inevitably past the old chemist shop on the corner, its brightly
coloured bottles unfailingly attracting my eyes. Sometimes the
door would open and unusual smells would catch my nostrils.
A strange, yet familiar feeling would sweep over me and a
longing to enter – I felt irresistibly drawn towards it. I found
myself seeking excuses to obtain purchases that were not really
essential.

The shop had been there many years. It was old-fashioned
and unadorned. Lack of paint and lack of money was very
evident. Despite its dilapidation it fascinated me, as it had an air
of mystery and age-old knowledge. It belonged to Edward
Smallbrook Horsley, MPS, nearly 80 years of age, and his
daughter, Doris Margaret. I would stay and converse with Miss
Horsley on many things. Of her father I saw very little as he was
usually engaged in the dispensary at the rear of the shop, from
whence came the intriguing smells. I always left with an
inexplicable feeling of excitement.

Exactly opposite, across the road, a young pharmacist had
started up with all mod. cons. and efficiency, no doubt eyeing
the quaint shop over the way, and his aged rival, with disdain.
This shop, with its modern tiles and smell of antiseptics, was
directly in my path as I journeyed home and would have been
the logical place to call, but somehow it repelled rather than
attracted me.

Although there was a great age gap, the friendship between
Doris Margaret and myself had grown. It was a very hot day.
Tired and thirsty though I was, I could not pass the door – the

mountain of toothpaste I was accumulating was about to be added to.

'Like a cup of tea?' asked Miss Horsley.

Readily I accepted and, joy of joys, I was invited into the sanctuary at the back. Poppy heads brushed my hair as I walked through. In the corner, a small apothecary's scale glistened. Phials and vials abounded everywhere. Strange names leapt at me from crowded shelves, all of which eventually I would investigate eagerly. Caryoph (oil of cloves), zingib (ginger, much loved and used by apothecaries down the ages) – there were fascinating names everywhere.

A tall figure unwound itself from the stool. It was Horsley himself, six feet four inches tall, gaunt but with a lovely smile. His grey eyes contemplated me warmly. My soul took two steps forward; it was instant recognition – I had come home. The cup of Brooke Bond tea I had been presented with suddenly turned into the nectar of the gods. The third eye was truly active, and if there had been a fourth, that too would have been working. Suddenly I noticed an unpleasant odour. I glanced suspiciously at the two cats sitting complacently in the corner. There seemed to be no need of interchange of words between him and me from the very first moment. The smile was in his eyes again.

'Smell this', he said, lifting the measure he was holding towards me. 'It's valerian.' The odour was like something a cat might have done. I then learned that, although the smell is horrible, valerian is a very valuable specific for nerve troubles and much used. The two cats were exonerated immediately.

It seemed inevitable that I would take up my abode with the Horsleys. The years the three of us spent together were halcyon days in which I absorbed – and reabsorbed – much, for it was as though I were relearning what I already knew.

I soon found myself swept into a maelstrom of little miracles. Three o'clock in the morning would find me still actively engaged in various experiments. There was a feeling of urgency in the air. Wartime had brought its problems. There was a shortage of oils for emulsions and sugar for cough syrups, and the allotment to pharmacists was based strictly on past usage.

In those days the huge alabaster pestle and mortar was very much in evidence. Most pills, emulsions and stock mixtures were made on the premises.

On Mondays, we made up the mixtures that would later be supplied to the many doctors in the area. This entailed the use of quantities of precious oils. Silent prayers would be sent up, as emulsions could be tricky and the tiniest mistake result in disaster. A day came when I was entrusted to make my first attempt. Laboriously, painstakingly, I obeyed, as I thought, all instructions. But, to my horror, I noticed that the emulsion containing precious oils had separated. Doris, seeing this, and my face, tutted sympathetically. Great soul as she was, she made no reproach. Instead she said kindly: 'It happens to all of us. Like a butcher, got to cut your hand once.' Somehow this did little to allay the despair within me.

'Naught you can do about it,' she said. 'Better throw it away.'

I just couldn't. 'Can we leave it for a while?' I asked, praying for a miracle. There was other work to be done, and I got on with it.

Next morning, on my way into the dispensary, I glanced immediately at the Winchester-quart bottle, but there had been no overnight miracle. My heart sank, but still I could not bring myself to throw it away.

That night was a truly Churchillian effort of prayer, blood, sweat and tears. My confidence had been shattered, and the wasting of the oils sat heavily on my conscience. Probably the understanding shown by dear Horsley and my friend only added to my sense of guilt. The dispensary had closed; everything was clean and put away. I finished my meal and wandered back in there. Suddenly a thought seemed to feed itself into my mind, no rhyme, no reason. I made an addition to the fated bottle, shaking it vigorously. That which followed was both unethical and unprecedented in the pharmaceutical world. I will not go into details here, but, when I discussed it later with my colleagues the comment was: 'You're certainly a trier, but it can't possibly work.'

On the Wednesday, I stood and gazed at the bottle before me. 'It's emulsified,' I told Doris delightedly. 'It's a perfect emulsion!'

She came over. 'But what can you do with it?' The addition I had made to the mixture rendered it useless for its original purpose.

Doris rubbed a little onto the back of her hand, as chemists do, to smell and appraise. 'Goes in beautifully,' she said. 'Feels lovely.' She tried some on her face; I thought her very brave. She was a most attractive woman, and rightfully proud of her appearance. Her eyes had the same qualities of warmth and depth as her father's but were almost violet in colour.

'Lovely face cream,' she said (there was a shortage at that time of cosmetics and lotions). 'Actually, it would make a good skin food.' We knew what had gone into it and we laughed.

'Could you make it again?' asked Doris.

'I think so,' I replied, secretly hoping so.

I could, and I did. We decided, in view of the demand, to supply it to the public. It had to be sold sparingly, for the oils were in short supply, but any excess oil whatsoever was channelled into the cream.

Then the feedback began to trickle in. A customer who had been treated by her doctor for eczema, without result, bought the cream as a cosmetic. She found to her joy that it was considerably helping the condition. So the story continued, and the cream began to establish itself. To this day, many little miracles later, the cream is still used in the clinic in which I later worked, and even more widely not only for its invaluable beautifying properties but also to help in the treatment of psoriasis, eczema and allied skin conditions. Amazingly, it was found that it did not need any preservatives as it seemed to be able to maintain its freshness. I have no scientific explanation. This was the beginning of many inspirations that, and I say it humbly, always seem to have come from a knowledge beyond ordinary knowledge.

Gradually a strange thing began to happen, for there appeared to be a reversal of roles between Horsley and myself. Now he would watch, fascinated, not trying to teach, but rather seeming to absorb what I was undertaking. Little by little the dispensing was given over to Doris, and I found myself spending more and more time producing the creams and lotions for which we had gained a reputation.

The time came, sadly, when Edward Horsley began his onward journey. I was with him, holding him, and we went to the very threshold together. Then he stepped over peacefully and with dignity. Doris and I missed him so.

There followed the heart-rending task of putting his affairs in order, and collecting all the papers and possessions carefully together. Somehow even the papers seemed to have a magic, a message from the man himself. Sitting on the edge of his bed, I found myself reading once again the indentures of his apprenticeship. They were dated in the late 1870s, so many years ago, when only the sons of gentlemen could afford the princely sum of £200 to become apprenticed. That was a veritable fortune in those days and I should guess represents at least £2000 or £3000 today. Horsley had shown me these papers some years previously and to my young mind the phraseology had appeared both intriguing and amusing. I noted once more the wording, and my mind flew back to that first occasion in the dispensary when my laughter rang out. I cannot give the words verbatim, but they ran somehow thus:

'I, Edward Smallbrook Horsley, do hereby agree not to frequent low taverns ...'

This had sent me into convulsions of mirth, for not only did I find the terms of speech archaic and delightful, but I could never visualize my dear Horsley wanting to visit such a place. I read on.

'I, on my part' (obviously the pharmacist training him) 'do pledge that I shall not feed the aforesaid Edward Smallbrook Horsley fresh salmon more than once a week.'

I confess that when I first read this my immediate observation was: 'Fresh salmon? Someone's joking, surely!' Fresh salmon was a real luxury to me then, as it is now. I was mystified. Horsley's patient explanation made it all very clear: 'You see, dear girl, in those days several apprentices would be resident with the pharmacist at the same time. We spent many years in training, often being allotted very menial tasks such as bottle-washing. Although the £200 paid to the pharmacist at the beginning of the apprenticeship was a large sum, there were no further payments. Thus the pharmacist's wife, with perhaps seven or eight hollow-legged boys to feed, sought a means of economizing on food bills. This was in the heart of Wales, remember. Meat was expensive, so what a boon to the house-wife was the local poacher, who would willingly trade a huge salmon for the humble price of a few pints of ale.'

The supply was unlimited and the poor apprentices were fed fresh salmon almost daily. The boys became so sickened by the surfeit of salmon that the situation became fraught with ten-sion, so much so that the aforementioned clause was written into the indentures.

And now, all affairs settled, the subject of the shop had to be considered. According to the pharmaceutical laws (which are still in operation today), it was illegal to dispense without a fully qualified pharmacist on the premises. Doris and I both ranked as dispensers, but although Doris was a member of the Apothecary's Hall and had been dispensing for more than 20 years, the law said that she could not run the shop as a pharmacy without the certificate of a pharmacist hanging on the wall.

It was always a problem when a pharmacist died, leaving the business to an unqualified relative. The practice was to employ a pharmacist, and generally it was a retired person who was most readily available.

Thus came Mr A into our lives. He was very elderly, jocular, obviously an inveterate gambler and, one vaguely suspected, enjoyed all the fleshpots of this world. Often, if one came upon him unexpectedly in the back of the dispensary, he would be studying the racing column and writing out his bets industri-ously, seated upon the same stool formerly used by my dear Horsley. Mr A's duties were not onerous, for in view of Miss Horsley's capabilities it was mainly for checking and verifying that we required his assistance. He would undertake the order-ing of stocks, so that weekly chore was taken completely off our shoulders which was a great help. For this we were duly grateful, and just paid the bills when they became due.

Mr A liked to have his lunch in the dispensary, allowing Doris and me to obtain our luncheon at a little place around the corner. As he was entitled to a lunch-hour, we insisted on closing the shop and locking the door until we returned, so that he could eat in peace. He was always most amiable when we arrived back and never resented the fact that sometimes we were just a little late. One day, while paying some bills, I noticed that one of the invoices was for a Winchester-quart of orange-flower water. Interesting! Orange-flower water was used by housewives mainly as an addition to the icing on cakes, and, as only the tiniest amount would be purchased at any one time, a Winchester would last several years. Vaguely I remembered seeing the old bottle with a considerable amount still left in it, so I assumed there must have been a sudden inexplicable run on orange-flower water. I paid the bill and thought no more about it. When, however, a similar invoice arrived during the following week I naturally concluded it was an error on the part of the suppliers and queried it with them, only to be assured that there was no mistake. I thought to myself, poor old boy, probably getting forgetful. He's duplicated the order. Never mind, I'll let it go.

That day Doris and I locked up as usual and set off for lunch, but on reaching the restaurant we found that owing to a sudden death in the family it was closed. Disappointed, we retraced our steps, thinking in terms of a snack at home. Doris unlocked the door and called out, 'We're back. Only us.' She didn't want the old chap to be worried by the noise of someone entering unexpectedly. There was no reply, so we assumed he was out at the back. Passing the shop counter on my way upstairs to the flat, I heard an unmistakable snore. It seemed to be coming from behind the counter. I made a little detour and there upon the floor, happily embracing a nearly-empty Winchester of orange-flower water, was Mr A in a deep drunken stupor. I summoned Doris.

'Well I'm jiggered,' she exclaimed. 'So that's where the orange-flower water went. He's been drinking it!'

We stood and laughed. Although we knew of the high alcoholic content of orange-flower water, drinking it as alcohol had never occurred to us. It became apparent that Mr A was an alcoholic. Unfortunately our association with him had to end there, for he now represented a hazard in the pharmacy. Incidentally, orange-flower water has a wonderfully soporific effect and is invaluable, two drops at a time in a night-time drink, as a treatment for insomnia.

Customers soon recognized the love and care that went beyond just dispensing, and learned to trust us. The shop began to become more prosperous. It was very clear that the cheaper, natural products would be recommended, and if necessary made up, rather than the off-the-shelf artificial or expensive branded goods. We were that which is sadly lacking today, the old-fashioned chemist and apothecary with whom one could talk and discuss problems as one would have, at one time, to a 'listening' doctor.

Affluence brought with it a danger of complacency. Sometimes in meditation at night, when deep called unto deep, part of me would feel what I can only describe as the Divine unrest. Within me there was the knowledge that this period of my life was only to be used as a learning and growing span, a time of reassimilation, and that in no way should I be tempted by the material gain and security brought about by my new-found affluence. This situation seems to be a pattern which has threaded its way through my life.

While still working at the pharmacy I moved on into the surgical world of chiropody which was really a continuity of all that had gone before. The instruments I used were but an extension of myself, an outreaching of love, caring and rapport with my patients. From the relative security of the chemist's shop I began my first practice. The practice grew. As always, in the midst of success came the Divine Nudge. I found myself, in the mid-Fifties, in the sweet little village of Great Missenden in Buckinghamshire. Again I was plunged into the struggle of a young practitioner without means of establishment, a testing time of faith.

'Kings Ransom'

The way 'Tiddington', a one-up, one-down former tithe cottage, came into my hands in 1960, when I was still a struggling practitioner in Great Missenden, was something of a miracle. I had first made the acquaintance of the hamlet Kings Ash when visiting a patient who was housebound. Her cottage, 'Tiddington', was situated high on a hill, 600 feet above sea level, with a panoramic view described in the guide books as the beauty spot of the Chilterns. It was completely surrounded by rolling farmland that dipped into the valley below. It was breathtaking. I loved my visits there and never left without longing to return.

When, sadly, my dear patient died, I heard on the grapevine that always exists in the country that the cottage was up for sale. My finances at that time were not particularly good – I was struggling to make ends meet after a spell in hospital for diabetes. The old saying 'if one does not work one does not eat' certainly applied. However, I felt I must find out about 'Tiddington', for the sheer beauty of it haunted me. Living in such a place had always been my dream.

I found myself interrupting my morning clinic, for someone had told me that the cottage would not be going through the usual channel of estate agents, but that a solicitor in Berkhamsted was handling the sale. Also, I had heard that several farm-owners whose land bordered the cottage had made what they considered very good offers for the property, desiring it for their farm hands. My heart sank. Nevertheless, I telephoned the Berkhamsted number.

Politely the solicitor asked: 'What is the maximum price you are prepared to pay?'

I replied that my absolute limit would have to be £800.

'A certain person has already offered well in excess of £1500', said the solicitor. That was a sum which, even if I had sold all my goods and chattels accumulated over the years, I could never have raised.

'Perhaps I may take your name?' concluded the solicitor. I told him who I was and how I had heard about the sale. I resumed my work, abandoning hope.

That night, seeking solace, I picked up my Bible and read from where the pages fell open. These words leapt at me: 'Every place whereon the soles of your feet shall tread shall be yours.' (Deut. 11.24.)

I got out my car. It was well past the witching hour as, with only the moon for a travelling companion, I drove up to 'Tiddington'. As I parked on the grass verge, I glanced down at the valley which lay bathed in moonlight. There was absolute stillness and an air of expectancy. I began to walk around the periphery of the land. I am certain anyone watching would have thought me completely mad. I walked round steadily, as with the walls of Jericho, three times. On leaving, I gazed up at the moon's face and I swear it was smiling.

That night I slept. My dreams were of the flowers that sprang up around my feet as I walked (for the land had become derelict), and of all the living creatures who danced in welcome. It was a magical night spent with elfins, fairies and flowers, surrounded by the animal kingdom. My soul was singing.

The next day came, and it was as if the night before had never been. Half-way through the morning the telephone trilled. A patient wanting an appointment? I wanted to keep busy. My faithful friend and housekeeper, Phyllis, who had been with me many years, picked up the receiver.

'Someone from Berkhamsted asking for you,' she called out. I hurried to the 'phone.

'Miss Wall? Is your offer of £800 still open?'

My heart pounded. 'Yes,' I said, wondering what was coming next.

'Well now,' continued the solicitor, 'a strange thing has happened. It has come to light that the owner of the cottage is the deceased's sister.' He went on to explain that she felt it would be wrong, in principle, to make excess profit from the sale, and that as she recognized my name and knew that I had attended her sister, she felt that she would like me to have the cottage at the price I had suggested!

'Can you get along here today, and bring a deposit?' asked the solicitor.

On wings I flew. I have no recollection of the journey there or back. Oh, thank you, Lord, I thought, thank you, thank you.

That night I gave my thanks standing on the borders of my home-to-be. This time I danced and laughed and sang, and the laughter re-echoed from the silent witnesses around me.

A year later I was struggling madly to save the then large sum of £200, the price quoted me by a local builder for restoring the now dilapidated cottage that it might become habitable. The fields and beauty around had not changed and many were the hours spent just digging, standing, talking and becoming part of the beautiful panorama that stretched limitlessly.

The practice in Missenden was growing. As I worked I would dream of the little cottage waiting for me. The day's clinic finished, the evening would find me planting and talking to my herbs and to the wild creatures in the fields. Phyllis, whom I have mentioned, my stalwart, had covered the ground with bulbs of all description so that the garden was beginning to resemble a miniature Holland. Even a small pond had been contrived, plus a crossing bridge where fools might tread, for its stability was much in doubt.

Wandering into the derelict house one day, I found two letters, both bearing the local council address. Planning permission had been applied for, via the builders, to convert the one-time lean-to shed into a garage, plus other minor additions. Had they granted permission? Eagerly I opened the first letter; the second one, I thought, was probably for rates. Permission had been granted, my dream was about to be realized. I had just reached the target, the £200 lay snuggly in the bank, and my first call when I returned home to Missenden would be to the builder.

My eye caught the second letter. Wonder what rates I shall have to pay? Better open it and find out. I stared unbelievingly.

Right at the top of the page I read the words, 'Demolition Order'. I turned the envelope over once more – it could not be for me. It was. 'Tiddington' cottage and my name were quite clear. It was crazy, or I was. In the same post from the same council came both planning permission and a demolition order!

The wheels of the car hardly touched the road as I sped back to Missenden. On the telephone the council corroborated the incredible information. The demolition order apparently had existed for 25 years before the purchase, and the council had now decided it would run a road straight through.

Frantically I tried to contact an old, well-established solicitor whom I knew was well acquainted with council ethics. He was not there, so an appointment was fixed with a newly qualified colleague.

The news he gave was not good. The earnest young face before me was full of compassion coupled with regret. A charming youngster, his sincerity shone forth from him.

'It is impossible', he said – as had many others – 'to fight the council. If there is a demolition order they are perfectly within their rights to execute it.'

My heart sank. I would have to accept this but my whole being cried out against it. I looked away from him, hoping my tears could not be seen. The pristine appearance of his certificate, newly hung, leapt at me from the wall. If I could have smiled at that moment I would have, for I remembered the day when my newly acquired certificate had been a matter almost of embarrassment. My eyes slipped down to the name 'Godbehere'. I drew my breath sharply. It's a sign! If God is here, why have I allowed my faith to be shaken? My spirits soared. I left, thanking him profusely.

My life has always been a silent prayer, communicating, through absolute faith, with a Higher Consciousness. However this is understood or interpreted by others, one of whom once asked laughingly if I had a hot-line to heaven, this is the faith through which I work and have been supported. It is the only way I know. I do not know what I have but I think it will become apparent that it is real and works. The persistent questionings – 'Are you clairvoyant? Are you this? Are you that?' touch no chords in me. That I am the seventh child of a seventh child, child of a man who lived in the same manner, I do not question, only accept. Were I to question every healing or foretelling that took place in pure faith I should never have time to do the real work for which I have been designated.

The night is long, detachment seems very far from me. My mind binds itself around my spirit, I hear the echo of the voices, 'It is impossible'. How many know this condition – the longing from the soul, and the mind that intrudes with cold reason! Three o'clock, the time of Samuel in the temple. Suddenly I behold a vision, something is twirling in front of me, silver, and yet with colours flashing. It is a sabre. Multi-coloured jewels gleam and dart from the hilt. It moves in circles and it is as if a spotlight is upon it. A sabre, I think. Of what significance is that?

I dismiss it, come back to earth and the hurt in my heart has not lessened. The second night the same thing occurs – the similarity between this occasion and later, the time when 'Balance' was born, will be noted as a pattern that occurs repeatedly throughout my life. The third night, and I hear the rattle. God must think me very dim, for it seems to have to be spelled out sometimes. The sabre whirls, there is a distinct rattle and suddenly the message is loud and clear: 'Rattle a sabre'.

Feet back on earth, puzzled by the strange injunction, my mind starts to tease out the message. What sabre? I haven't a leg to stand on, let alone a sabre to rattle. I laugh silently. Perhaps it refers to me, to rattle my brains. I search for the true meaning of rattling a sabre.

During the morning clinic the figure six shillings and six pence occurs again and again, tapping itself into my brain as if on a Divine keyboard. It conveys nothing tangible, nevertheless I know I am receiving somewhere a 'Divine Nudge'. This is a lesson long learnt.

Evening, and I wearily pick up all the correspondence regarding 'Tiddington'. One piece of paper detaches itself and falls to the floor. It is the copy of the official search, made on my behalf by the Berkhamsted solicitor dealing with the purchase. The fee stated for this service is the official charge – six shillings and six pence. My heart contracts. My eyes devour the paper. These words burn themselves into my brain: 'THERE IS NO ROAD PLANNING OR DEVELOPMENT SCHEME IN PROCESS.' And it was signed by an official of the council. Distinctly I heard through the throbbing of my head the rattle of the sabre.

A further appointment is made with Mr Godbehere and we discuss the point I have seized upon. The eyes across the desk view me earnestly.

'Shall we rattle a sabre?' I ask. 'Surely this is an official error which has placed me in a predicament? It is false information that could leave me homeless. I have already sold all I have in an endeavour to purchase and have agreed to vacate the premises I work and live in.'

'We'll try', he said, smiling suddenly.

I lobbied local councillors and the residents' association, and there was no rest within me until the day came – against all odds – when for the sake of six shillings and six pence 'Tiddington' was saved. 'Tiddington' was eventually renamed 'Kings Ransom', for that is exactly what it was all about.

In June 1964 some time afterwards, I met Margaret Cockbain, who was established at Amersham as an osteopath, and immediately we recognized and admired the quality of each other's work. By 1970 we had decided to merge practices at Amersham and to live together at 'Kings Ransom'.

Each morning the clinic would be dedicated by Margaret and me before we started work; the whole atmosphere was one of peace and harmony. There was a rapport between the patients and ourselves, and complete trust. With pride I recall that we had been entrusted with three generations from all walks of life, all equally loved and cared for. The practice grew over the years. Margaret was joined by three other osteopaths, and I added three chiropodists to my staff. We were very careful in our choice of practitioners, so that the quality of the service provided at the clinic was forever constant. Both Margaret and I centred our lives on the clinic, and leisure hours were very few.

As finances eased, it became possible to extend and improve 'Kings Ransom'. Because of the beauty of the surroundings, Margaret and I indulged ourselves by having huge picture windows installed wherever possible. From these windows in early morning one could observe the clouds and the mist riding up, like stallions in the sky. We had been told that, at night when the house was aglow with lights, viewed from the valley it looked almost like a lighthouse or a glass tower. It was a fairytale palace set in a perfect landscape. 'Kings Ransom' was truly the only name that could be given, for the place was beyond price.

The few precious leisure hours in the evening would find me standing in the garden, breathing in the aromatic perfumes of herbs and sweet essences of flowers around me, flowers and herbs I had planted and which became the essences and extracts I began to use in all my healing creams and lotions.

Slowly I would make my way to a gap in the fence and step through into the field. There I would stand quite still that I might not disturb the little creatures going about their various tasks. Somewhere along the hedgerow a pheasant would cough impatiently, searching and calling for his spouse, late in returning home. No doubt he was mindful of the fox who was ever watchful for easy prey. The birds, busily preparing for the night, would be chattering agreeably or, in some instances, disagreeably as they settled their various families. Standing silently, sometimes one could see for an instant the rabbit leap before disappearing into the corn, or a small wild deer, for which this area was noted, bound into the undergrowth. Suddenly I would be drawn back to the time when, as a child clutching my father's hand, I wandered amongst the flowers, herbs and the wild life that he loved so. Somewhere deep inside me I knew there was something still to do.

Time to Stand and Stare

What is this life if, full of care,
We have no time to stand and stare?

William Henry Davies

Late in 1973 came another 'Divine Nudge'. Whilst on holiday in Majorca, an isle that proved to be ill-fated for me on more than one occasion, I had a huge coronary which disposed of much of my heart's function. I was close to death. Margaret waited patiently at the hospital for three or four days as I fought for my life. Gradually my condition improved and I was flown back to England to receive further treatment at a local hospital.

Upon my return home, I was carried upstairs to my room and told that on no account was I to try to tackle the stairs for at least three or four months. Desolate and weak, I resigned myself to life in a bedroom. An inner voice told me that I would be well again when the daffodils appeared, and in this I put my trust.

My bedroom had a huge picture window, practically the width of the room, which looked out on green meadows and fields of waving corn stretching far and away over the patchwork quilt of the countryside. The first field was just a few yards from the house and bordered the garden. The boundary was marked by an almost invisible wire fence, giving the illusion that field and garden were one.

Lying in bed, I had time for reflection and observation. During my busy clinic life, this peace and solitude was something I had longed for. Now I had been granted it, though not as I would have wished. Visitors at this time were not permitted. Margaret had transferred her patients from the clinic and saw them at the house, for I could not be left alone for long. Apart from the regular check visits from Margaret, I was isolated. I had all the time in the world. So what an event it was when the farm cart trundled down the lane, or the tractor chugged by my window on its way home after a busy day in the fields!

The daffodils at last arrived. As they heralded the warm spring days with their cheerful yellow trumpets, so I began my slow and tedious struggle back into life's stream.

I had been advised that I should graduate towards a three-mile walk every day, to build up strength in the remaining undamaged heart muscles. In the first week, in triumph I walked up the lane to the first tree, no more than a hundred yards. I had little control over my legs; my knees tended to buckle without warning. Reaching the tree was a tremendous relief. I rested a while, my body supported by its broad trunk – my first 'tree hug' in months – before turning and labouring back. Gradually I progressed, tree by tree, forcing myself sometimes, for the body had not yet grown accustomed to its depletions. Eventually, again with that Churchillian effort of 'blood, sweat and tears' known to me throughout life, I reached my goal: the distance of three miles.

Although the lane was rough and unmade, passing a solitary farmhouse and two tiny cottages, it was a beautiful walk. Cows followed me with their soft liquid-brown eyes. I spoke to them gently, and gave each a name. Occasionally, one would shadow my footsteps for the length of the field. Pheasants calmly crossed my path with all the confidence in the world, for their time had not yet come. Here and there a hare would bound through the field. I was now outside enjoying what I had viewed only from the inside.

The Divine Nudge had been a warning. But how often did I need to be told? I had been instructed that there was other work for me to do, that I should move on and out into a new direction. Six months had now passed since my heart attack, and for the first time in my life I was ignoring the Divine guidance. I was refusing to move on. Perhaps because I was nearing retirement age, and having had so many setbacks, I hardly anticipated another move. Already my mind was reaching out to my return to the clinic. It was now a well-established practice, with our patients reaching third generation level. I loved them all. Even leaving aside financial considerations, the temptation was to return.

I felt ready to resume my work, although I was still rather weak, for the coronary in conjunction with diabetes had depleted me considerably. It had been an arduous struggle back, but I refused to opt out.

One Sunday morning I sat in the kitchen finishing my cup of tea prior to my walk. Idly I watched Margaret chop a huge onion on the draining board by the sink. She was using one of those mechanical choppers where one bangs on the top and the chopping action takes place underneath. The sharp, metallic blows, like pistol shots, seemed to shatter my ears, sending an unbearable pain darting through my head and eyes. I put my hands to my head.

'Stop banging. Please!' I yelled. But Margaret, deafened by the noise, did not hear me and continued with great gusto. It lasted only a few seconds, but to me it was an eternity. When the banging ceased, I took my hands from my face. As I opened my eyes and tried to clear my vision, a huge red 'butterfly' appeared in my left eye. I tried to clear it by blinking. It would not go. It seemed to grow larger and larger. I became alarmed. Margaret, fearing a detached retina, quickly telephoned the doctor. We were told to report to the surgery. After being examined, I was sent directly to the hospital with a letter.

It was not a detached retina. It was a massive haemorrhage which completely blocked the vision from that eye. 'The only medication is time,' the doctor said. The haemorrhage did eventually resolve itself to some extent, but the sight in that eye never returned.

I left the hospital in a turmoil. Perhaps because of my weak state, or perhaps because life had always shown this pattern of struggle, I felt utterly destroyed. At what seemed like the moment of triumph over difficulties, at the peak of recovery I was thrust back once more into nothingness. It seemed too cruel, more than I could bear. I walked away from Margaret as we reached the cottage. The rain had started falling and it merged with my tears as I walked and walked and walked, blindly, not caring where. Margaret, understanding my agony of mind, left me for a while, then followed in the car. It was a time of battling with myself, the first time I had ever felt like giving up the fight.

But later I came to know that this episode was for a purpose, to give me time – time to settle my affairs and get used to the fact that, with partial sight, I could not continue at the clinic for much longer.

I bought a huge, American-style magnifier and with its help went on working. I had worked very much by feel and inner knowledge even when I had full sight. My fingers had always been my eyes, therefore I had an advantage. God was good.

Now, with the doctor's warning still ringing in my ears – that the other eye might deteriorate – I began my 'blind' training. Deliberately I would close the right eye as I performed various everyday tasks, deliberately walking a short distance with both eyes tightly closed. Thus I learnt to rely more and more on the sensitivity not only within my hands but within myself. I was preparing, and being prepared, although not fully understanding why, for a future need, teaching myself to know my own space.

It was 10 long years later that we learnt from another consultant that there is a fragility left within the blood vessels for quite a time after a coronary, and that excessive noise could bring about what happened, especially where there is already a weakness. I mention this that others may be aware of it, and act accordingly.

However, I was adequately compensated by what was to follow. A change began to occur in me. With the lessening of physical sight, a new dimension in auric awareness (i.e. seeing auras) came flooding in, almost to the point of pain. It began to take precedence over all other faculties, while every sense within me seemed to be sharpening.

Although from childhood onwards I had the ability to see

auras, which was the gift of my lineage, the full significance of this had not been understood by me. In fact, ever since the incident in childhood at the age of eight when I had been taunted by my schoolmates, it had been a secret hugged silently to me. An aura sighting would occur without warning, at any time, perhaps in the middle of a conversation. Always I would dismiss it lightly, fearing. But the gift had stood me in good stead, giving discernment in situations when deception was present.

Now, thrown back as it were on this gift, in human contact there was no pre-judgement to cloud the issue. Words, clothing, appearance, all were of no importance; nothing could distract me from the true person within. When the aura is viewed, the millionaire is on a level with the roadsweeper. Both are stripped of all outward presentations. Earthly standards vanished from my vocabulary. Before, people were to me 'as trees walking', but now I could see 'every man clearly'. (Mark 8.24-25).

Looking at and talking to people was now such a different experience. I was fully aware of their emotions, their thinking. I knew the man without guile, the cunning in the eyes of the devious. I began to know their silent thoughts, and their needs were ever before me. While conversing casually, I would suddenly find myself sighting them as far back as the beginning of time, sighting their attire, who and what they were. It would be of a moment, like the flicker of a candle flame. Sometimes a whole scene would be experienced and, on occasion, it could be very disturbing. An in-depth conversation with a person would sometimes reveal that his problem of today had its foundation in his past which I had already observed so scenically. Thus, the ancient scribe I had seen momentarily could well be linked with this present lover of words who, at this moment appearing almost inarticulate, has yet to express his own thoughts through the power of the written word.

This above all: to thine own self be true.

Shakespeare: Hamlet

The Road to Damascus

It was early in 1979. The little port of Andraitx in Majorca had never looked more beautiful to me than it did at that moment, with the sun aslant the waters breaking into a myriad of colours.

Carefully I picked my way past the nets spread on the quayside, past smiling mahogany-faced fishermen who sat cross-legged, mending the nets. One was busily peeling potatoes into a bucket, presumably for the midday meal. They were well acquainted with me, and I with them for Margaret and I had been staying there for a month-long holiday and during my daily three-mile walk along the promenade their glances had passed from natural curiosity to friendly acceptance. I had gone a considerable way when, silently, Margaret fell into step beside me. It was a routine we followed. Margaret did the shopping first, joining me for the last part of the journey back. Almost immediately she touched my arm and pointed. There in front of us was a sudden spiral of tiny silver bodies in the water. High in the air they leapt, small fry being chased by some bigger fish. For one spectacular moment it seemed almost like a hand held up in greeting, or farewell. We laughed delightedly, standing by the rail, and the next moment they had gone. We continued on our way unhurriedly, stepping as near the water as we dared, watching the sailors on the boats at their chores. Every moment was precious for we were just two days from returning home.

Abruptly I stopped and stood still. My hands went to my eyes urgently – it was as if, when driving, a lorry had thrown up mud onto the windscreen as it passed, obscuring vision. Margaret glanced at me.

'I can't see,' I said quietly, controlling my voice.

'Something in your eye,' said Margaret.

I made no answer. It will go in a second, I thought. It did not. Cobwebs of blackness were moving about in my eyes. I put my hand through Margaret's arm. This was most unusual, for I preferred walking with arms swinging freely. We were very close, so I felt Margaret's puzzlement.

'I can't see,' I repeated. 'I can't see.'

In stunned silence we returned to our apartment, this time avoiding the fishermen and their nets for they now constituted a danger. It was the last time I was to see Andraitx.

We decided there was no point in returning home early as our flight was booked for only two days later. I think, secretly, we hoped the affliction would resolve itself. It did not. After a while, for a brief period, there was a slight improvement and a degree of peripheral vision still remained. Nevertheless, this final blow meant severance from the clinic and my work as a chiropodist. God had slammed the door behind me in preparation.

Gold Hill

With my sight problem added to other health complications, it soon became apparent that Margaret and I could not continue at 'Kings Ransom'; I could no longer drive and help was hard to come by. Reluctantly, we resigned ourselves to an enforced retirement, and began to look for a convenient bungalow, small enough for us to manage on our own, and where there would be easy access to shops and people. My God-given 'Kings Ransom' was now to be passed on. We chose carefully; it was never a matter of the highest bidder. Rather, we sold the house to a patient whom we knew was God-centred and who loved it.

We had an affinity for 'leafy Bucks', and had no intention of going too far afield. It happened that Phyllis, my faithful friend and ex-housekeeper of 30 years was about to retire from her little shop in Chalfont St Peter at the top of Gold Hill Common. The flat above it was spacious and looked out over the common. The vast expanse of green gave the impression of the farmland we had enjoyed at 'Kings Ransom'. The flat had been empty for some time and was in need of repair. It would need a considerable amount spent upon it, but there was a lovely feeling of peace and prayer. It occurred to us that it would suit our needs – the only real obstacle, the stairs, could be surmounted by installing a chair lift. Phyllis was delighted. We were to be together again.

We planned it all very carefully. A door was fitted in the bedroom leading out onto a flat roof, and there we built a garden patio. Here I could lie in bed with the door open in the summer and imagine myself once more in the garden I loved. Margaret hastened to plan and plant. Sweet peas, honeysuckle, clematis, wisteria – all took their place on the tiny roof garden.

It would soon be a blaze of colour and a sight to behold. We prepared for a quiet retirement, having decided to invest our capital, our whole life savings, with a friend. We planned to live on the interest, for our needs would not be great.

Our morning meditations were spent on the patio, a veritable sun-trap, where the mind and spirit could very easily take flight. The walks I had always done were continued, no longer along a farm track but on pavements surrounded by woodlands. These walks were a time for spiritual 'walk-about', and a means of reaching up into Higher Consciousness. A beautiful avenue of trees marked part of the walk. I would bless them as I passed, and was blessed by them.

Each day now settled into a retirement pattern with its usual filling in of time. Then came the Divine discontent. The curtailment of the physical could in no way impair the intense and immense longing for a deeper knowledge of the spirit. At this time, we heard of a spiritual group of people who met regularly at a nearby farm. They embraced equally all religions. We decided to go and meet them.

The auras among the group were varied but lovely. One aura, with its beautiful soul spiral, made me catch my breath – Laura. She stood in the doorway smiling. It was instant recognition, for we had long been acquainted in the eternal circuit, and our souls took two steps forward to greet each other. Margaret and I decided it would be right to join them.

The farm rented by the commune lay in beautiful countryside. Like most centres, it was perpetually in need of funds for its upkeep. Wishing to make some sort of contribution, I offered to supply some of the creams and lotions I had been making for over 40 years, for use in our clinic. I now found it difficult to pour the creams, so I asked the group for a helper. There was silence. I saw the auras, in varying degrees, flicker.

Laura asked gently, 'Why do you need a helper?'

'To fill the bottles,' I said matter-of-factly.

'Oh,' said Laura, and burst out laughing. She then explained, amidst general laughter, that a 'helper' in Subud meant an experienced member chosen for his or her ability to guide others when in difficulties. Always a practical giver, Laura said:

'I'll help you, Vicky.' And from there it all started.

The cream had always been made white for clinical use. 'Could we have it in a colour, to distinguish it from the ones at the clinic?' asked Laura.

'Any colour you like,' I answered. 'I'll make a full range for you to choose from.'

I enjoyed myself immensely, and soon found myself enveloped happily in the colours. Seven appeared under my hands and I placed them proudly in an arc to view.

'What a perfect rainbow,' said Laura. 'Can we have them all?'

So began the rainbow creams and lotions. We made our first dozen or so, and these trickled out through the farm members. Laura then suggested we start a little enterprise. This idea had been fostered by the Subud leader, Bapak, who encouraged initiative and enterprise among the members.

Out of the blue came an offer to Laura of a stand at the Subud World Congress at Windsor, to be held in August 1983, where a spectacular complex would be opened by Bapak. It was to last two weeks, and at least two thousand members would be arriving from around the world. This was a far cry from the few bottles distributed from the farm. We were now talking of several thousand bottles to be prepared.

Lincoln Fraser, Laura's husband, known to us all as Mick, decided he would come in with us. The four of us called the venture 'Lincoln Fraser Products'. Although I knew it would represent a great deal of work, I accepted the challenge readily. The opportunity of once more using my age-old and instinctive knowledge through the medium of my creams, lotions, herbs and essences was something I could not disregard. I remembered the day in the old dispensary when the creams that were to prove so valuable were first conceived. I felt excited. Inactive retirement was absolutely impossible, and blindness held no bar. That which lay deep inside me needed to be expressed, and I felt I was being nudged back into life's stream again. But the vastness of the Divine plan had not dawned on me. I had no idea that this was the culmination of what I had been destined and trained for since the beginning of time. 'Balance', as yet unknown to me, was about to be born.

The day of Congress's opening loomed. Time was short and 'getting it together' was a mammoth task. Mick was busy with his career, Laura did not enjoy the best of health and had to have a spell in hospital, and Margaret was not too well. I made all my creams and lotions by hand, the formulas were known only to me, and now we were intending to produce many thousands of bottles. Without my sight, the pouring and labelling was beyond me. So we had to get help from whomever we could enlist.

Despite all this chaos, the Great Authority decided that the miraculous oils should be born. Their time had come. I remember the quote from Omraam Mikhaël Aïvanhov, discovered in ancient treatises on alchemy:

> . . . *a certain oil containing miraculous properties that could not only cure illness, but give one power, wisdom, beauty, this oil is made of the subtlest elements contained in the sun's rays. it has been given all kinds of names — Prana, the Elixir of Eternal Life, magnetism . . .*
>
> *In the future this will be a part of a whole science that will be studied.*

The Night 'Balance' was Born

Where have you come from, baby dear?
Out of the nowhere, into the here.

George MacDonald

Deep into a week of crisis, with unlooked for pressures and deadlines to meet, I sought for peace and renewal within my meditations. That night my meditation turned out to be weird – but wonderful. After I had achieved the earthly detachment necessary, I found myself suddenly enveloped in a most beautiful cascade of colour which advanced and receded like the ebb and flow of the tide, sighing softly as it went. As it came towards me, rhythmically, I longed to remain within it. My whole being was suffused with vibrant new energies and peace. The peace that passeth all understanding had flooded me entirely. The third eye had opened fully; the world with its commands and demands was no longer with me.

Then came the still small voice that I had listened to and obeyed so many times before. It came as if from the hollow of a cave.

'Divide the waters, my child'.

'Divide the waters?' I came back to earth with a thud. What waters? I dismissed it as a trick of the imagination, suspecting that I had gone too high.

The second night was a repetition, with the same injunction, 'Divide the waters'. Once again, mystified, I came out of meditation quite quickly. On the third night I began to feel like Samuel in the temple, for I could no longer ignore the voice, even though the commonsense part of me said: 'What are we thinking about? I'm not Moses. I'm blind, only 40 per cent of my heart is working, and I'm well into my sixties. Who would I be leading into what promised land?'

But I had to pay heed, and I got out of bed. I do not remember the next few hours, nor how 'Balance' was actually born; I only know that other hands had guided mine.

Next morning Margaret asked: 'Whatever were you up to last night? And just what are all the lovely bottles for?'

'I don't know', I said.

'Then why did you make them?' queried Margaret, with her usual practicality. 'They must have a purpose.'

The breakfast table is not usually a place where one wishes to go into details that seem weird and inexplicable, although I knew Margaret would have been understanding. We continued to eat in silence. My spiritual walk-abouts would take me, on occasion, well into the night, so I needed to eat and earth properly before discussing anything. Furthermore, I did not understand it myself. I needed my morning ruminative walk and silent communing, within which, I knew, something would be revealed. I had faith that the whole matter would be fully revealed to me when the time was appropriate. That there was a message and a purpose I had no doubt.

As if drawn, I entered again the tiny room downstairs in which the birth had taken place. We stood and stared at each other, the bottles and I. They gleamed brilliantly in the sunlight; there was a serenity about them and a power seemed to emanate from them. The liquid in each was in two layers. These layers lay gently one upon the other, sharply divided, and usually the upper was of a colour different to the lower. Was it imagination or were strange sensations passing through me? It seemed as if there was almost a communication between us, for something within me was resonating. Suddenly I felt energized and happy. The physical tiredness I had been feeling lifted, as if magically. The name 'Balance' came into my mind, as if it had been whispered. 'Balance' had been born and she was beautiful. But still the question 'What's it all about?' that Margaret had voiced seemed to find no answer, and what 'Balance' was to become was still, as yet, a mystery.

This has often happened and I believe it is a method of Divine testing for me. I receive the instructions first, but the meaning is shown later, after the act of obedience.

Once I started to put together my coloured jewels I seemed impelled to make many variations, each one seeming to have its own vibrations. It was as if I worked under some strong compulsion, and various combinations of colours began to form under my fingers. I was completely absorbed by them.

Time, however, was not on my side. The Congress was only two weeks off. Literature and labels had to be produced. One thing, at least, I was certain about, knowing the natural contents, that it was, whatever else, a most perfect beauty oil after the style of Cleopatra and her asses' milk, a lovely balance of moisturized oils and plant essences – the first, I believe, in this era.

That it was also a re-emergence of something I had knowledge of in the far distant past I have no doubt about whatsoever. Gradually the full meaning and the structure began to make itself known. It was a continuation; all was so familiar and was pouring into the consciousness. The old wine had appeared in a new form in 'new bottles', expressly for the New Age.

When asked – and repeatedly I have been asked, particularly by the people who must always measure and quantify – how long this had been researched, my reply is this: 'It has been *re*-searched for a very long time, back into the very beginning of time, and then searched, re-searched and re-membered.'

Thus went out the inspirational oils that were later to amaze and astound many. I was immersed in the time track of past knowledge, not fully understanding but letting it flow, letting it happen.

Congress

The first day of the Subud World Congress dawned bright and fair. The stand we had been allocated was situated within a huge marquee, near one of the main entrances, and I noticed that the tent flap had been fastened back. I gave silent thanks, for I have always had a fear of enclosure, no doubt a relic of some previous experience. It was August and the sunlight streamed through the aperture.

We set up the stand as best we could, without the expertise and props of the professionals around us. In fact, all we were provided with was a trestle table over which I had thrown my mother's white linen sheet, now a hundred years old. This, together with one long pane of glass filched from a friend's shop upon which the bottles were to stand to give them height, constituted the presentation. Laura's son-in-law had painted a picture for us, according to our visions, and it stood at the back of the stand. Whatever the venue, this picture has accompanied me ever since, and has always attracted admiration and comment.

Around us, the professionals had excelled themselves. Drapes, placards, pamphlets, all the devices that large companies could command were there in force. Amid this grandeur, our small stand resembled the local voluntary agency's stall, to be found most Saturdays in the high street, selling home-made jams and goodies.

Laura and Mick, having undertaken much of the bottle-filling and labelling beforehand, were to join us later. So with my lack of sight, the main setting-up was left to Margaret. I suggested, as we had no other props, that the pane of glass should be positioned on top of some 'Balance' bottles we had discarded because of their cloudiness. These bottles were the result of an attempt to reconstruct the first, inspired batch, but although I had made, as I thought, a complete replica in colour and substance, the result proved disappointing.

Two or three people trickled in and one woman paused at our stand. The sunlight formed a natural spotlight at the back of the stand, illuminating the 'Balance' bottles. They seemed to vibrate and gleam, the colours brilliant and strikingly beautiful. The woman appeared to be fascinated. A sale, I thought. But no, slowly she moved on and disappeared through the aperture. A few minutes later, to my surprise, she was at my elbow.

'I've been looking at the bottles at the back. I don't know why, but I'm drawn to them.'

She did not ask about their purpose and there was nothing on the stand to indicate what it was, for 'Balance', as stated before, had emerged just before the start of the Congress.

'Could I have that one?' she asked, pointing to one of the rejected cloudy bottles supporting the glass shelf. Its counterpart stood above it on the shelf, beautifully bright and clear. I concluded that she had not noticed the latter, and, since my training would not permit me to sell or give anything that I felt inferior in quality, I steered her to the clear bottle.

'Take it to the light,' I said, thinking that once the sun struck this bottle there would be no contest. But she returned, saying apologetically, 'I would prefer the other one, if you don't mind.'

Setting up the pane of glass on its props of cloudy bottles, then placing the ones for sale on top, had proved hazardous and time-consuming for Margaret, since the tent was pitched on a slight incline and the legs of the trestle table were none too steady on the turf. I struggled with a feeling of exasperation, but this was our first customer. I smiled to myself. Typical woman, always thinking the item right at the bottom of the pile is the best! I glanced over at Margaret. Her face was expressionless. Painstakingly, all the bottles were removed and the pane of glass lifted. The woman had her bottle.

'Thank you,' she said. 'I felt I just had to have this one. It's almost as if it spoke directly to me.'

There was no crush of customers yet, so I escorted her to the exit. 'Enjoying the congress?' I asked conversationally.

The woman looked at me. 'Well, I hope I will.' There was weariness in her voice as she continued: 'I made the effort to come. I'm just recovering from a breakdown.' I tut-tutted sympathetically and she passed out of my sight.

Margaret rebuilt the stand. Six times during that day came a demand and insistence upon purchasing a cloudy bottle. I was puzzled. Customers were also buying the creams and lotions, as I thought they might. But some seemed irresistibly drawn to the cloudy 'Balance' bottles at the back. When asked what the bottle was for, I could only reply that it was a beauty oil, which at that time was all I understood. As I have said before, I have learned to obey first, knowing that the answers will surely follow. Ours not to reason why, but I do feel that the Divine has an excellent sense of humour.

Customers were still sparse, for many people had only recently disembarked from their flights at Heathrow and were drifting in casually, perhaps feeling the effects of jet-lag. With a desire to enjoy a little sunshine, I accompanied them to the exit, asking the usual question: 'Are you enjoying the Congress?'

I elicited one strange fact. The six people who had chosen cloudy bottles had all been through a recent depression or emotional crisis. Thus I concluded that perhaps in some weird way the cloudy bottles were picking this up, or were significant to the person's needs. I mentioned this to Margaret. With her practical mind she immediately responded: 'Perhaps we ought to make a survey of this. It must have some importance.'

By the end of the day, we had exhausted the small supply of cloudy bottles we had brought with us. But since people were still requesting them, and were resident at local hotels, we offered to bring along further supplies.

During the fortnight, all 140 cloudy bottles went out thus. It had become such a regular pattern that we began to have the confidence to ask the purchaser: 'Have you been going through any emotional upset recently?' We found with unerring regularity that it was so. Oh well, I thought, God knows who needs it most.

On the final day a bright young man came up. There was by

this time a crowd around our stand, for many little miracles had happened. Four of us were serving flat out. The young man picked out two bottles while he was waiting in the queue. To my surprise, he had chosen the last cloudy bottle, the one hundred and fortieth, and the equivalent brilliant bottle. As he stood there, he picked them up, put them down, then he left to peer anxiously through the doorway, as if checking on something. He returned. But again he seemed undecided, picking up first one bottle then the other.

'I don't know', he said, 'I'm drawn to this one', pointing to the brilliant bottle, 'but I feel as if I resonate to this one' (the cloudy bottle). He settled for the latter.

Margaret asked brightly, 'How are you enjoying the Congress?' Although he seemed so cheerful, she obviously expected the usual response.

'Oh, fine', he replied. 'It's great. I've never felt more settled, satisfied, or so happy in my life. I am doing the work I have always longed to do and I feel complete.'

Margaret and I looked at each other. 'Bang goes our theory', I said softly. Margaret persevered.

'What is the work you are doing?'

But the young man was craning his neck to peer outside where a small boy was patiently waiting. 'Oh, it's all right', he exclaimed, 'he's still there.' Then to us he said, 'I am working with mentally retarded children.'

The bottles had spoken.

The Congress was now rolling, with two thousand visitors every day, a truly cosmopolitan cross-section of society. Many of the parties were accompanied by interpreters, as several groups spoke hardly a word of English. Needless to say, this led to quite a few complications in communication.

Our stand was now surrounded, mostly by women who seemed attracted to the colour and beauty of the bottles. I became aware of a tall figure (this I distinguished by the aura colours way above the others). I could feel a concentration, and that it was a man. He remained for a few minutes, obviously looking at something, then disappeared through the opening. He soon returned to the same spot, rapt in thought. This little performance I 'observed' at least three times before lunch.

Lunchtime came and we split up, for the stand could not be left unattended. I chose to wait. Suddenly a huge figure loomed beside me. The aura was very familiar. It was the man again.

'I'll have that bottle,' he said, 'the blue one. How much is it?'

I told him. He paid, placing the bottle in his jacket pocket. Intrigued and mystified, for he had asked no further questions, I gently enquired: 'Would you like me to tell you how to use it?'

'Nope,' he said, 'no need. I know exactly what I'm going to do with it.'

He moved as if to walk away. By now, I was not only puzzled but a little peeved. It was my beautiful baby, and I wanted to know what would happen to it. He must have caught the expression on my face, for he laughed out loud. All the people I had met there were lovely people, as was this man. I learned later that he was an agent for a large assurance group, in charge of their gigantic stand at the far end of the marquee.

'OK, I'll tell you,' he said. 'All morning I've been coping with awkward questions, interpreters and the like. I felt that if I didn't take a break I'd blow my top! As I passed your stand, with the gaggle of women round it, something at the back caught my eye.' (It was the blue 'Balance' bottle.) 'It seemed almost personal to me. Sounds crazy, eh? But as I stood, a peaceful feeling came over me. I went outside, then as I came back past here the same thing happened. I returned to my stand to meet the same situation, but I felt calmer. I dealt with the problem, and I got the business! The peace didn't last long, the pressure was on again. I escaped, came back here – same bottle, same fascination, same effect. Third time round, I thought, when those blessed women disappear, I'm gonna get that bottle! And you know what I'll do with it? I'll put it on my stand and just look at it. Then I'll take it back home to Canada and keep it on my desk.'

This was the first spoken evidence of the visual therapeutic qualities of the blue 'Balance', which became known as the 'peace' bottle.

The Congress was sited well away from the town centre, which made it difficult for many visitors to visit the shops. Consequently, they took full advantage of what was on offer at the Congress, and our little stand was no exception. By now, the word had spread and we were becoming the focus of requests for help. These people were highly spiritual, very much on the higher level, and they believed in natural healing.

The woman hovering behind me was sending out signals of excitement and love, like rays that penetrated the back of my neck. I turned to face her. She took my hand and held it as if she would never relinquish it. There was sincerity in her voice as she said: 'I'm so grateful for your help.' I waited, wondering what was coming next. 'Thank you for healing me.'

Apparently, she had long had a painful cyst on the side of her eye. Gradually, it had grown until it interfered with the opening of the eyelid. Because of the position of the cyst, she had feared to have surgery. She went on to tell me that she had purchased the 'Rescue' oil (which at that time had no name) and had been applying it to her face purely as a beauty oil, as instructed in the brochure. By the fourth day, the cyst had miraculously disappeared. I was not sure whether she was crediting me with the healing, or the oil, or both, but naturally I was very pleased for her. For the remainder of the two weeks, she haunted our stand, eagerly insisting on helping us in any way she could. Her gratitude knew no bounds.

A man who asked me 'Can you recommend anything for impotence?' was drawn to the red and gold oil. He staggered away at the end of the session with 30 bottles. There must have been a good time had by all!

My next visitor had a very different problem – a severe abscess the size of a golf ball on her buttock. To Margaret's amusement, I was conducted to the back of the marquee and asked to 'take a look' at the abscess (a term lightly used, I feel, with my physical disability). But by now people were fully convinced that I had an inner vision, and it was this they came seeking. From an orthodox medical viewpoint, the size, feel and heat emanating from the abscess suggested immediate lancing, followed by a course of antibiotics. The woman was ill and feverish. In the act of anointing, I felt drawn towards the blue and violet 'Rescue' oil. Gently I placed the oil upon the abscess, holding my hands there for just a moment so that the oil might be absorbed. I passed the bottle to her. 'Put some more oil on later', I said, thinking it would help sooth the area until she was able to obtain medical aid. I made no charge for that bottle, it was given with love.

Next day a girl came and thanked me for her mother's miracle. 'The abscess burst last night, and now we are bathing it and clearing it, then putting on your healing oil. My mother is so grateful.' Then she added, 'Could you give me healing?'

I began to wonder what it was all about. Were they attributing these happenings to me, or the oil? I was not sure, but when subsequently people began to buy the 'Rescue' from someone else and still the miracles continued, the doubt was cleared away.

From then on we were overwhelmed with people returning to thank us. Unsought came the reports. Migraine headaches had ceased after the 'Rescue' oil had been applied, lumbago eased and backs bent in pain for months were starting to straighten after the all-gold oil had been used. My dear Laura had fallen badly on site, and had been rendered unconscious for a short time. All we could think of later – and Laura felt this for there can be no disputing her affinity with the Infinite – was to use the yellow-on-gold 'Balance', which worked admirably. With this gold oil came a double bonus – the digestive troubles that some visitors from overseas had experienced, perhaps because of their change in diet, were also remedied. The list grew longer and more amazing each day.

Margaret and I discussed it. We were bewildered. I could not believe what I was hearing – I had, so to speak, gone to switch on a lamp and had lit up the whole of London. The real miracle, I believe, is that I had never read a book on colour therapy, nor studied the rules of colour composition. All that had been done, as with the cream, had been done as if other hands were controlling mine. It would be much more acceptable to the media and to the 'men who must measure' if I were to claim years of research (as they understand the word). But in fact, I had been taken back to the beginning when God said, 'Let there be light.' And there was light. And light was the life force and the beginning of the life energies, and there I 're-searched' and thus, remembering, entered the mysterious and magical world of colour in the Greater Garden of God.

Operation 'Lift-Off'

The enterprise name 'Lincoln Fraser' had served its purpose, acting as an overture to the main theme – Aura-Soma 'Balance' and its healing mission. The name Aura-Soma had revealed herself in meditation and was corroborated by Laura when 'testing'. *Aura* is derived from the ancient Greek and is represented by Aurora, goddess of the morning light. *Soma* in Greek means 'being', in Sanskrit, 'living energies'. Thus Aura-Soma is 'the light made manifest in living energies'.

Offers of financial support began to pour in. Advertising executives approached us, and a world-famous cosmetician was interested in backing us. I found myself refusing all offers. 'No thank you', I said, 'God is my banker'. At that point I was certain God smiled. The great test began.

Becoming aware of a potential we had not dreamed of, the four of us discussed the matter in depth. My visionary Laura and I knew full well that this was no accident and that there was a depth far beyond anything we humanly understood in what we had been given. The temptation to succumb to financial bidders was not within Laura or me. I was adamant. Divinely inspired, blindly obeyed, the Divine hand that had led me back in time was literally to lead me forward in faith. It was tantamount to a mission. Nothing would persuade me to reduce 'Balance' to a mere cosmetic. Its sheer beauty was just an outward means of attraction, God's shop window as it were, and all who cared to look in it would find a mirror of the true self and its needs on many levels.

Franchises were suggested from all around the world – and refused. A woman approached me, fascinated by the coloured 'jewels' spread out before her.

'You must market this!' she exclaimed. 'It's the first of its kind. It only needs advertising in the right places. I'd love to handle it.' Her face was alive with a radiance that seemed to reflect the scintillating colours she was gazing at. I liked her.

'Advertising is my business,' she continued, 'but I feel personally drawn to this.'

My mind, which had flickered at the word 'business', fell into focus again at the obvious delight within her. We were in the midst of dismantling the stand now and there was no further time for discussion. As we were about to depart, she came up again and said, 'Can we talk about it?'

'Yes,' I said, and Margaret arranged a future time, address and date.

Nothing as yet had been formulated within our minds. Events had happened so swiftly, so unexpectedly that no plans for the future had been made. But of one thing I was certain: until a full explanation in God's good time had been given to me and the real purpose of this mysterious, magical substance been revealed, there would be no selling out for commercial reasons only.

Margaret and I had invested our capital – the sale of 'Kings Ransom' plus our life savings – with a friend, thereby securing, we thought, good interest upon which to live comfortably. There was no desire or incentive for us to enter the world of commerce. In the furtherance of this little miracle, the financial aspect did not seem of any importance, except in so far as it could bring the true purpose of 'Balance' into being. Secure in this knowledge, we were prepared to proceed with whatever presented itself.

Reports were still coming in of healing, on the spiritual, physical and mental levels. Strange things were happening within me. All my life I had been conscious of having an inner vision and pre-knowledge, along with inexplicable feelings and intuitions. There had also been spontaneous, unsought healings. But now all these had been increased and released a thousandfold. Colours, sounds, perceptions came in with razor-sharp clarity, perceptions beyond just mere perceiving. It was as if 'Balance' contained a release mechanism transmuting and transmitting the liquid, live energies from within itself, bringing in a higher level of awareness.

'God's my banker.' I heard the words echo and re-echo in my mind. I gazed blankly at Margaret. We had just received the news that our investment had failed. Not a penny could be recovered. Blind, retired, and in my middle sixties, I felt far from optimistic. Thank God we had already prepared and moved into my faithful Phyllis's flat. At least we were not homeless. We had spent lavishly on comfort and refurbishing before the 'crash'. God was certainly taking me at my word and testing faith. That night in meditation I asked the question 'Where do we go from here?' The child of inspiration had been born to become, as I thought, the saviour of many and we could not even afford the swaddling clothes.

Next day the woman in advertising came as arranged. I looked at her glowing face. The excitement was still there.

'I've used it,' she said. 'It's fabulous. I just felt inspired and centralized, as if I had reached a new direction. I've been thinking about it – in fact, dreaming about it!' She laughed. 'I know exactly which magazines, at least two or three, I could get it into.' She paused. 'I know it would cost considerably more, but it would have to be in colour.'

The word 'cost' penetrated. For a brief time I had thought this lady and her offer of handling advertising might have been God's answer – help had been asked in meditation. But cost had not been mentioned. Somehow, as we had never really thought of it commercially, the idea of paying for advertising had not occurred to me. In view of the recent financial shock, the realization that we were talking money brought me up with a jolt. Somewhere at the back of my mind a thought flickered. Perhaps with the sale of certain private possessions we could raise a few hundred pounds. The importance of advertising was not lost on us. The biblical cry 'How will they know if there is none to tell them?' was imprinted on my mind. The mission was ours; it had to be fulfilled.

'How much are we talking about?' I asked softly. 'Would it be very costly?'

'Oh no,' she replied, 'about £7000 should do it.' She sipped her tea happily. I choked on mine.

'Well, honey,' I said, 'we don't have seven thousand pence so I'm afraid we've got to sit this one out. Some time maybe.'

After she left in the late afternoon, the gloom descended outside the house, and inside. I must admit that at this point God's sense of humour was lost on me. Advertising would have to be forgotten.

On the advice of a friend we had invited Simon Martin from the *Journal of Alternative Medicine* to see if we could interest him in our new discovery, the therapeutic qualities of 'Balance'. I was determined that these should not be lost and that our beautiful 'Balance' should not end up merely as a cosmetic. The telephone rang. It was Simon. Yes, he would like to come but could only manage a Sunday. That would be fine, we said, delighted. Was this the answer to our prayer?

On Sunday morning we prepared the dining table and produced our best. A fire glowed. It was early January and a biting easterly wind blew over Gold Hill Common. The phone rang – Simon again. Could he bring a friend? Certainly. Hastily we laid another place.

When the doorbell finally rang my heart pounded. Please God, let it be right and give us inspiration. It could mean so much! As Margaret opened the front door, the wind nearly blew them into the hall. Londoners, unused to country cold, they shivered. Upstairs it was warm, the table inviting, but somehow intuitively I knew I was not receiving a response from either of them. My heart sank. Words, words, all seemingly empty – we were getting nowhere fast. Downstairs in the garden room where 'Balance' had been born the bottles were laid out and waiting in all their beauty. To reach this room entailed passing once more into the cold outside air. As they entered, they shivered. I despaired. It was going to be a waste of time.

Suddenly I felt a change in Simon's companion. She was handling the bottles as if almost reluctantly drawn, seemingly unable to leave them alone, held by some irresistible impulse. Her questions were abrupt, penetrating. I began talking to her. We were now discussing my beloved baby. Information poured from me. It was sheer love that spoke. That she was just an interested spectator did not detract from my enthusiasm and joy of sharing. Simon seemed untouched.

We saw them to the door. Simon sensed our disappointment. Cheryl, his friend, turned suddenly and kissed us. The warmth surprised me, although I knew of a past link between us. My heart lifted, though this had nothing to do with the reason for their coming, just the sheer pleasure of a person to person contact. The outcome seemed of no consequence. Margaret and I had little hope of a free editorial, judging by Simon's reactions.

A few days later, Margaret was reading the morning post. The last letter in the pile caused us both to sit up straight. It was a glowing letter of thanks, not only for the hospitality but for the beauty of information shared.

'I would like to write an article about you and 'Balance' for *Here's Health*. Would it be possible to send a photographer to take pictures in colour?' The letter was signed Cheryl Isaacson. Our hearts sang – we had indeed entertained angels unaware.

The colour photographer duly arrived, a highly-professional young man who, much to our interest, produced props like handkerchiefs from a magician's hat. Bright umbrellas appeared, strange contraptions hung here and there, some to stop light, some to give light. It was such a complicated affair. My beautiful 'Balance' bottles just beamed and winked away at the photographer as he focused.

A further letter arrived. The article would be published in three months. It seemed a long way off.

Hard on the heels of Cheryl and the *Here's Health* feature came another telephone call. This time it was the brilliant author and journalist Leslie Kenton from *Harpers and Queen*. Could she come on Sunday? Talk about never on a Sunday – everything seemed to happen to us on a Sunday.

'We'd be delighted,' I said. Would we mind if she brought a friend and her small son? The pattern seemed pre-ordained. An evening meal this time and another welcoming fire. I prayed silently that yet another fire would be started.

The meal over, we descended to the garden room. From the moment of impact, no hesitance here. Fascinated, drawn through the inner knowledge of past awareness, her selection of colours confirmed what I had already seen within her. About to embark on a special article on exposure to colour, this was to her an entirely different dimension. It was truly a first of its kind, startlingly beautiful and referred to by Leslie as resembling jewels from a child's fairy tale. Her son, Aaron, a most intelligent child, seemed equally attracted. Certainly here was a boy who one day would bring much colour into many lives.

My auric vision wandered to her friend in the background. His aura had been immediately known to me and recognized. Memories from the past rushed in. Here was a great soul indeed. I drew my mind back to the present situation. Leslie eventually departed bearing several of the 'jewels' with her.

Confirmation of Leslie's article came later. It also was to be published in three months' time. Margaret and I looked at each other. Heigh-ho, I thought, this indeed was 'lift-off'.

The photographer from *Here's Health* who had been such fun called in casually on his way to another client nearby. We had issued an open invitation for him to drop in for tea if ever he was passing. Answering our enquiries as to progress, he said: 'I think Cheryl's done you proud. You're getting a full double-page spread in colour.' He grinned. 'That would have cost you if you had been advertising.'

'Oh, how much, do you reckon?' I asked.

'About £7000,' he replied.

I drew in my breath and looked across at Margaret. The same thought leapt into our minds – £7000, the same impossible sum suggested by the advertising agent. And on top of this had come the extra bonus – *Harpers and Queen*. God indeed was a generous giver.

Olympia

The Body, Mind and Spirit Exhibition held at Olympia in the summer of 1984 was the first really big exhibition at which we had a stand.

The bottles gleamed under the lights, flashing their message of promise for the future. Suddenly people were crowding around, almost hemming me in. I found myself inwardly looking into the faces of very old souls and friends. There were those with whom I had walked, talked, taught and learned throughout the various reincarnations. I was travelling back through time into timelessness, since God had first said, 'Let there be light.' And there was light, and with the light came life and through the prism of life itself the spectrum of colour was revealed, each facet with its own specific wavelength and vibration, and its own healing qualities.

So many of us there had known the whip upon the back, the flames at the feet, the sword at the throat. Since the day of ridicule on my eighth birthday when I had started hugging the 'secret' in my hand, I had fought against speaking about such things. It was now 60 years later and my father's words rang in my ears: 'The day will come when you will be able to stand up and tell of this gift.' Not only was this a time of open declaration and recognition but also of a complete awareness of the true purpose of the inspirational coloured oils. With the failure of physical sight had come a powerful inrush of inner vision. The auras that I had always been able to see now had a clarity that enabled me, as it were, to look through the windows of the soul, rolling back the curtains of consciousness so that I might see all aspects of a person, and his or her total needs. It was strange, exciting and disturbing. I was now wholly subject to the Higher

Consciousness that guided and worked through me. There was complete emptying of self.

My lovely Laura, with her deep inner sight, had said at the very beginning: 'There is a purpose in this far beyond and quite different from what we see immediately.' In many ways one could say that she was the instrument of a Divine push. All her predictions eventually proved accurate, and her support, faith and encouragement, as well as her envy-free nature was a true source of strength to me.

Many souls pulsated and vibrated at our stand, a truly born-again time. It occurred to me that a great teacher had once said: 'Unless a man be born again he cannot enter the kingdom of heaven.'

Many tears were shed at my little table, of relief and recognition. People were coming from the four corners of the earth, not by chance, but called, a mighty army, missioned and commissioned for the inbringing of the New Age, prepared by the past for the present.

A second's lull at my table, then a young woman's voice at my elbow: 'I represent ——. Are you talking about colour and its effects on people?'

'I am.'

She went on: 'I've very little tape left. Would you please answer as briefly as possible.'

I watched with interest the aura in front of me flicker and deepen into brown at the periphery. I observed the unbelief within.

The clipped voice continued, 'You say colours affect people. I'm wearing blue. What does it do for me?' A microphone was thrust into my face. Not much, I thought, and was tempted to say so.

'It should provide the peace you so obviously need,' I said 'No doubt the job you do and the pace you work at must make that very difficult.'

This was not, apparently, the answer she wanted. The voice hurried on: 'All right, suppose I wore green, then what?'

'Green,' I replied, stifling a sigh, 'helps decision-making, polarizes, gives a person the ability to find the space he or she needs. I call it my go-hug-a-tree colour.'

The microphone was speedily withdrawn. 'Thank you,' she said, and passed on. I never heard anything of that interview, nor wished to. From my pocket I drew out my 'Pomander', the essence of Aura-Soma (see pages 159 and 160), and with a gesture now internationally familiar cleansed the air around me. I added two further drops on the palm of my hands, outspread in silent oblation to the seen and the unseen, cleansing the vibrations around, protecting the aura from external sapping and wrong elements.

The 'Pocket Pomander' was to become much loved by all those engaged in the New Age healing of the multitudes. It proved invaluable at the exhibition. We were happy to hear that the atmosphere at the exhibition centre seemed very much lighter that year.

At lunch a smiling Laura came up to me. It was our first chance to speak to each other since we started. I had been pinned to my table, either by the press or by people asking for personal readings, and had had no time to appreciate what was going on at our main display stand where Laura, Margaret and the others were working. 'I must tell you, Vicky, you'll be interested,' said Laura. 'I noticed this man standing in front of our rainbow spectrum of bottles, holding out his hands towards them for several seconds. I didn't approach him and he moved away. This happened several times and I became curious. I thought perhaps he wanted information but didn't like to ask. I approached him carefully, asking if I could help. "No thank you, dear," he replied. "I'm just regenerating when I feel the need."'

Laura added: 'He comes from the next stand, one of the spiritual healers. It didn't help our sales, but they are doing wonderful work next door and I'm glad we are playing a part in their healing.'

It was beginning to dawn on us that visually the colour and other vibrations emanating from the bottles had a restorative power. In fact, friends who have known me for many years have remarked on the personal rejuvenation that has taken place since I have been handling Aura-Soma.

Then came another voice at my shoulder. This one was

spiritually alive, warm, excited and with an accent I found hard
to place. The eyes, the windows of the soul, were alight and held
a deep inner awareness.

'Would you please explain to me the full meaning of what you
are doing and what this is all about?'

No shortage of tape this time! Here was a kindred spirit and,
in spite of the crowd, I made the time available. Eagerly every
word was recorded and now and then a pertinent question
posed. It was a delight. Half an hour later, we had only just
finished. The young man asked permission to photograph my
oils in colour. He had with him only a black-and-white film at
the time, but the next day he reappeared and we rearranged the
stand so that he could do justice to the jewel-like bottles. (The
subsequent pictures we saw six months later in the Danish
magazine *Nyt Aspekt*. They were beautifully and sensitively
done by Steen, the young man who had interviewed us. The
article itself, of course, was written in Danish – tantalizing that
we could not understand it until translated.) Before Steen left
the stand, he invited us to exhibit in Copenhagen the following
year.

Two weeks after Olympia, the stand was re-erected at the
Alternative Medicine Exhibition in Kensington. This was a still
wider field. Therapists of all kinds crowded around, as if drawn
by some magnetic force emanating from the Aura-Soma stand.
These were dedicated New Age workers, absorbed by the
ancient arts of healing in its holistic aspect – hypnotherapists,
acupuncturists, radionic experts, reflexologists, aromathera-
pists and many more. There was the occasional enquiry from
an allopathic doctor or an interested nurse.

This time the questions asked were deeper and wider. They
were concerned with the full structure of Aura-Soma, and its
effect on the physical as well as the mental and spiritual. I found
myself speaking about a format which hitherto had been contained only within my own consciousness. It was all beginning
to come together, and now a whole concept within the spectrum had appeared. The words began to flow, the floodgates of
memory had opened. I was once more the teacher, reliving and
remembering. Notes were being taken, questions asked. All

those present were resonating to something which was not alternative to what they were presenting but an exciting adjunct, offering a widening of their field. They were realizing that Aura-Soma was not just colour therapy, depending on the healing vibrations of colour, but a powerful, newly resurrected old concept that held within it the ancient alchemy of the apothecary wherein lay the secrets of field and forest – the herbs, the flowers, the resins.

A tall, dark young man asked: 'I'd like to know more about Aura-Soma. When are you having a workshop?' It was then that I became aware of a need for a fuller teaching. There was no doubt about this, for by the end of the exhibition we were inundated with names and addresses from all over the country. The workshops born from this exhibition were eventually to spread beyond Great Britain to Europe and the New World.

Copenhagen

In November 1985, many exhibitions later, we went to Copenhagen for the Body, Mind and Spirit Exhibition to be held there. This was our first big venture abroad and the obstacles were many. There was customs, with its endless documentation and form-filling. Then arrangements had to be made to transport the oils and exhibition stands in a separate vehicle by land and sea while Margaret and I travelled by air, for sea travel was impossible for me. We found it hard to devote all the time needed to organize the trip, as the demands now being made upon us were many. At one stage I wondered if we would ever overcome the problems, if we would ever get there. But direction had been given, and in meditation I had been told I was to go.

Margaret and I landed at Copenhagen airport in teeming rain, a reminder of England. A hurrying figure approached. I stepped forward to meet her, for the auric vibration I was receiving told me this was our hostess. We embraced, and immediately my soul settled. Ulla is a truly wonderful person. She and her husband Erik were the most perfect hosts. With their delightful daughter Anna, a chiropractor of great repute, and their son whom I was to meet later, they formed a united, sweet-souled family. Their home became our home during our stay and was, too, for Michael Booth and his wife Claudia, who had come along to help me. They had travelled by car, bringing all the Aura-Soma products and equipment. I had met them at an exhibition at Malvern in 1984 and they had invited me to give a seminar at their home near Glastonbury. The following year Michael decided to join me full-time. He and Claudia are my spiritual son and daughter, great healers in perfect harmony.

On the first day of the exhibition, we had just completed erecting the stand with all its paraphernalia when the lights were switched on. Immediately the magic started. Standing there, I felt the same warm glow that a mother might feel in the midst of her family, each one with its own personality, each making its own contribution in the circle of love.

A huge bright light suddenly appeared, and a tall figure loomed over me.

'Would you like to talk to me?'

'Do you speak English?' I asked.

I could feel his smile, and came his lovely reply: 'Do you speak Danish?' I loved him immediately. Suddenly I saw the arrogance of my question.

'No,' I replied, 'I'm ashamed to say.'

We smiled at each other. A few of the usual questions followed, and the now familiar personal question: 'Can you see my aura?'

'Yes,' I said, holding up the gold and red bottle first. This was, in fact, his chakra reflections (his need, denoting the colours he should have for his life-style requirements) rather than his aura colour – the red for energy, and gold, the need for wisdom to channel it positively. His 'true aura' colour was blue in essence. Interesting, I thought, for one day perhaps this man, who probably held a secret ambition, would realize it. I shook the bottle and the sunset flared in front of me. Oblivious of the light, now lost in the vibration, I whispered: 'Isn't it beautiful?'

'Yes, it is.' He stared intently at the colours.

I had become accustomed to cameras photographing the stand, but this little episode, I was amazed to learn later, had been filmed for television and was shown on a weekend television programme.

The exhibition was now in full spate. Not only was the stand lit up, but I too could feel the force around me. I knew why I had come to Copenhagen – the city was seething spiritually. Those who visited the stand were people with a calling, New Age people. These were Atlanteans, inward-looking, with deeply regressed eyes that had seen so much, and quiet voices that said so little, finding it hard to relate to the space and the people around them. Their chakra colours and auras showed clearly their need, the need for the element of water, the sea, and to immerse themselves in it. Many of them suffered from mineral deficiencies and dehydration. They all responded immediately to my Seaweed Mineral Bath, with its sea elements so necessary to them; it was almost as if it was natural for them to touch it. Subsequently, for we were there for several days, many an Atlantean remarked on his complete re-energizing after using the Seaweed Bath.

I found it interesting that the aura predominant among the Atlanteans was turquoise – in fact, any combination of blue and green was automatically chosen by them in 'Balance'. I realized that here was a peak of Atlantis and that these Atlanteans had followed the course of the ocean. It occurred to me, after the exhibition at Copenhagen, that this was the largest assembly of Atlanteans I had been privileged to meet. Again, they were powerful healers, relating immediately to the blue/violet 'Balance' now used and loved by healers around the world. Some, as yet awaiting their full power to come upon them, held out their hands to receive the essence of Aura-Soma, the precious 'Pomander', upon their outstretched palms.

A hand is thrust before me, and suddenly I am aware that here is one who had walked with the Master Himself. Immediately, I am told in reply that she had had a vision of the self-same experience. From that moment, knowing her true self, she goes forward in full power. Yet another, coming in from another planet, a space-healer, whose aura appeared with a deep violet and gold combination, the periphery almost star-shaped in its outline, looked at me with seeking eyes. I spoke of what I knew about him, and as we talked, much as we had done in the remote past, the aura flickered and changed, becoming slightly diffused with green in the centre. He was now beginning to relate to this space, the here and now, the New Age on earth.

Another aura shimmered in front of me. Here was a special one indeed. We touched hands, we touched souls, we knew each other. She had travelled all the way from Italy, not really knowing why, and then came to Denmark to attend a workshop that she might obtain a mirror and a shop window through which people could see reflections of their own beings and potentials.

Many were the tears shed at our little stand, many were the recognitions shared. It was so exciting, so exhilarating, and I knew then why it had been necessary for me to come to Copenhagen. I knew also that I must return again. Before we left, offers poured in from everywhere, houses were opened to us. They hungered and thirsted for knowledge.

I accepted an invitation to hold a follow-up workshop in Copenhagen the following April. This was to be repeated again and again at the Roskilde home of Annemaria Jeppesen. A wonderful hostess and a teacher of dance who became one of the first exponents of a vision I had had, the dance of the chakras.

Last year I was invited to give two lectures at the Healers for Peace World Congress at Elsinore. TV cameras were there and I was given a two-hour radio programme. The response was overwhelming.

If I am allowed, on my borrowed time, I shall return yet again to Copenhagen, that glorious city with the mermaid and the promise for the New Age future.

Colour Magic

Colour therapy *per se* is one of the most ancient therapies, stretching back into the mists of time. Researchers throughout the centuries have acknowledged the profound influence of colour upon the physical, mental and spiritual well-being. Each colour component of light has its own wavelength and specific qualities of energy capable of affecting the whole gamut of human emotions. For example, blue is a peace-maker, yellow uplifts, red can change inability to positive action and green can stabilize and centre a person to improve self-esteem. Similarly, the effects of colour on human health have long been established. Primitive man knew the use and meaning of direct application of colour, and its powers, spiritual, mental and physical, were well understood by him. Evidence of this is being found even now in ancient tribal caves with their coloured drawings. This was primitive man's first spiritual and physical expression.

The first-century Roman physician Celsus used coloured skin plasters to help promote healing. Today, Japanese researchers find that blue speeds recovery of wounds in animals. In the Middle Ages different coloured rooms were used in the treatment of various ailments, and many of today's hospitals and children's homes continue the practice.

In America, Indian braves who used war paint did so for a purpose. Each colour had a specific use, and was mainly to give their enemies an illusion of fierceness in combat, or to weaken the resistance of opponents. Yellow was for promoting strength and courage; blues and greens gave them ancestral support. Does not this strike a familiar note today, with the female putting on her 'war paint'? Red lips invite life; blue or violet eye-shadow give the impression of mystery. Beauty is not skin-deep. It is dependent upon many aspects of the whole body (soma). Influenced by emotions and physical conditions, it is the shop window for the true inner being.

The First World War saw the use of colour for shell-shock treatment. Colour is also medically recognized in antiseptics and healing agents – for example, gentian violet, magenta paint, crystal green, and acriflavin (yellow).

From the scientific angle, with Aura-Soma 'Balance' oils we are working through the medium of colour wavelengths. The rays of the invisible ultra-violet and infra-red are used by the orthodox medical profession. It is always advised, however, that protective measures be taken when ultra-violet is used because the high frequency of the rays can be damaging. Infra-red rays have a lower frequency than that of red lights and manifest as radiant heat. By using colours through the medium of 'Balance', we synchronize their wavelengths to the wavelengths of the body's electromagnetism. This is an absolutely safe therapy, and so the valuable vibrations of colour can be placed in the layman's hands.

The human aura is an electro-magnetic field, seen by clair-voyants as coloured rays emanating from the spine. Russian scientists have discovered that there is a predictable physio-logical response when colours are applied to a blind person. It is always found that when one sense is lost, eyesight for example, another sense becomes more fully developed than normal. It is through such a sense – be it of vibration or any form of sensation – that any person can determine his or her identity colours (see page 90).

Auras today are being depleted by atmospheric pollution, resulting in physical and mental repercussions. These emana-tions can actually be seen by specially gifted people. However, every person is instinctively drawn to his or her auric colours (these can be single or plural) and can thus recognize his or her own needs. Aura-Soma 'Balance' was evolved for just this purpose.

Aura-Soma 'Balance' seems to have a magic of its own. It appears to relate to the personal needs of the individual. For some the power is purely visual. For others it acts as a personal barometer, reflecting like a mirror the moods, situations and physical needs of the moment. There is a feeling of living energies supplying when there is demand. The chameleon qualities of 'Balance' have puzzled many.

I was amazed one day when a former patient and enthusiastic user of my creams and lotions phoned and said: 'Miss Wall, I'm puzzled. I took my yellow-over-gold oil with me on holiday, as I always do. While in Italy, I took it out of my case and to my astonishment the gold had turned green!'

'I reckon you needed space,' I commented.

She promptly replied, 'I'll say I needed space. It was the day feelings were running high against the British. Our coaches were being stoned and in danger of being overturned.' This sort of thing defies rational explanation. But the fact is that changes do occur when certain situations arise.

Here is another example which, viewed from the standpoint of common sense, could sound like nonsense (nevertheless, to what sense does it relate?). It was lunch-time. The telephone rang. An Aura-Soma enthusiast was calling from her place of work. She so adored her 'jewels', as she called them, that she polished them every day. 'Something has happened to my bottles, Vicky. They were fine half an hour ago. Now they're all bubbling like mad. I haven't even touched them. What does it all mean?'

I hesitated, feeling slightly apprehensive. Not wishing to alarm my friend, I played it down: 'Sounds like a bit of turmoil somewhere – just a day for taking care.'

She seemed satisfied with that, and I resumed my lunch. Two hours later she rang again.

'I thought I'd better tell you. The police phoned me to say our house had been burgled. A neighbour reported it, but too late; the culprits had gone. When I got home, I found they had taken all our personal valuables.'

It is interesting to note that the bottles did not cease their agitation until the culprits – some young people she had befriended – were caught.

Margaret, being down to earth and medically trained, found

it hard to accept the significance of such phenomena. So did I, at the beginning. But then Margaret observed in her own bottles a marked change whenever she was under stress or fighting an infection. When shaken, the oils went cloudy, a thick congested effect with no sign of her normal brilliant energy bubbles. After the infection or stress had passed, her oils resumed their norm. Margaret is now convinced that the change is caused by a vibratory response within herself.

The coloured oils, containing plant essences and extracts, in their crystalline bottles seem to act like a 'dowser'. There are so many amazing facets – fascinating, mysterious, inexplicable. As one handles the 'Balance' bottles, the desire to go deeper becomes almost compulsive. Many Aura-Soma therapists are using them to make in-depth studies. Through 'Balance' their own inner consciousness can work and relate, and so it is a means of diagnosis on a completely holistic level taking into account body, mind and spirit. I feel that one of its purposes is to serve as a warning system, alerting the person involved to take precautionary measures.

Those in tune with higher vibrations find there is a dream symbolism which can be interpreted within the Aura-Soma 'jewels'. Since the earliest times dreams have always been looked upon as a source of prophecy. The interpretation of dreams was deemed of major importance in biblical times. The riddle is: When does a dream become a vision?

A question I ask repeatedly is: 'Do you dream in black-and-white or colour?' Nightmares, some of which are flashbacks in time, bringing the old fears into the present, are practically always black-and-white, acting as a negative of the positive. Coloured dreams usually concern the immediate or the future. Remembering the black-and-white ones could well be a psychological guide, perhaps helping the individual to better understand the fears and hang-ups that infiltrate his 'here and now' and increase the deeper knowledge of self. To be 'fulfilled' is to be truly aware of the real self since the soul began its spiral journey.

Visions, prophecies, foreknowledge of all kinds seem to come in colour. Some references to colour in the Bible could well have a deeper meaning than is at first apparent. For example, in the Old Testament one reads of the coat of many colours given by Jacob to his son Joseph, an act of such importance that it created murderous envy and hatred among Joseph's brothers. Was the spectrum of colour an indication of a special spiritual gift? It was the same Joseph who later foresaw through the Pharoah's dream of seven sheaves of golden corn that a storehouse of corn must be prepared in Egypt for the coming seven years of drought.

How 'Balance' is Used

The Aura-Soma 'Balance' system is simple to use. It works through all the levels of being. On the physical level it works through the chakras, the energy wheels known to clairvoyants and yogis. If any of the chakras are stressed or weakened, physical, emotional and sometimes psychological disturbances arise. For each chakra, there is a 'Balance' bottle, specific to the organs, muscles and glands governed by that chakra, that will help restore the energy flow. Full details of these are given in the next chapter. Not only does the 'Balance' system act as a barometer of physical and emotional conditions, it is informative of past, present and future events. Above all, 'Balance' provides a mirror for the soul, giving knowledge of the true self which, once revealed and understood, can be healed. As I like to say, truth is that which is revealed to a person when the 'searchlight' is turned upon it.

And ye shall know the truth, and the truth shall make you free.

John 8:32

Before describing in detail how the 'Balance' bottles are used in diagnosis and therapy, I should like to relate an incident that occurred when I was speaking to a group of people in Israel. As usual, the oils had created great interest, and people had even followed us back to our hotel. Margaret and I took supplies of Aura-Soma everywhere with us, because we knew by now that wherever we went there would be requests for help – the magnet of healing drew many.

One day, by invitation, we met a mixed group of enquirers at the house of an interested person. It was a friendly, social crowd. Some had already used the oils. In such a cross-section of society, inevitably there was one who 'needed to measure'. The man, a scientist, had found the blue/green oil worked for him. Having listened to what I had to say, he posed the familiar question: 'Tell me, what's the magic? I know it works, but why? What's the composition?'

There was a hint of superiority in his voice and I noticed that the aura was tinged with brown, which is usually an indication of one trying to 'tune-in' through the intellect alone, which I refer to as 'going into a brown study'. It was literally colouring his thinking, but I recognized that he was genuinely trying to understand. Often I have found, especially with sensitive souls, that there is an inner blockage barring the way to complete fulfilment. They stand on the brink, teetering, unable to take the plunge. They feel their security lies in their intellect rather than in their intuition. How satisfactory it is when the block is at last removed and one sees the emerging of a powerful soul in full flow.

'I can tell you the composition,' I said. Instantly I felt the mental pens and papers coming out among the assembly. I smiled inside. Such a statement was much looked for in any such gathering, for the prospect of knowing something that was perhaps commercially viable naturally aroused great interest.

'I can tell you the composition,' I repeated. 'It is very simple.'

I drew my mind back. I regarded the enquirer with love, recognizing the true seeker. His wife was with him and his son and daughter, a close-knit, loving family. His hand rested affectionately on his wife's shoulder and they were bonded together, as it were by a devoted child on either side. The wife's aura was almost identical to her husband's, but with a feminine variation to it. They were indeed soul mates. I lent towards them smiling.

'But before I tell you, shall I tell you your composition? Were we to talk of you, or your wife, your son, daughter, friends, you all have the same physical composition, which isn't magical or amazing – so much water, blood, bone, fibre, salts, and so on. That is the composition of everyone in this room. But what did you fall in love with as a young man? So much water, bone, fibre? No, you fell in love with the "true aura" of your partner, the soul, the essence that you recognized and to which you resonated. And did you not bring colour into each other's lives? The body and its composition is merely the temple in which dwells the eternal self; it is an encasement for the true harmony of the soul.'

He nodded slowly in agreement.

I continued: 'It is what goes beyond the composition that creates the magic, and on that level the mirror of love, as in healing, is revealed, and it is you, your soul, a true light, that makes the miracle.' Now he was with me and so were those gathered around.

My ability to see the colours within people as a representation of their true personality had been with me since childhood, but I had never discussed my auric sight with Margaret or anyone else. Margaret had always regarded my ability to recognize the real person behind the presenting person on a first meeting as a gift of discernment, biblically described by St Paul. We found it a great help when employing staff and Margaret had learned to trust my instinctive judgement.

Through much observation of people visiting our stand at the first exhibitions, I discovered that the aura colour I was seeing intuitively, through the 'inner eye', was almost in every case the first 'Balance' colour that they selected. It seemed that when faced with the Aura-Soma 'Balance' range – the mirrors – each person selects his or her own true reflection. Thus it becomes apparent that auric knowledge is latent in everyone. This is not really surprising. After all, we have all been 'with ourselves' since the beginning of time, and therefore know more about ourselves than anyone else, even though it might be on a super-conscious level. Instinctively each of us chooses the colour of our aura and intuitively knows what our body needs.

Even a severely mentally handicapped child is able to choose his aura colour. This to me is really wonderful, that such a child, unable even to say his name, can find his identity in the wonderland of colour and light from whence he came in the beginning. Somewhere in this handicapped child is the light of memory, and that has not changed from the beginning of time, and that is the one means of contacting him.

I noticed that in harmonious relationships, one partner would choose the same colour or one of the colours of the other person. This applied also to children. In the case of twins, the same colours would be chosen even though neither knew the choice of the other beforehand.

To begin a consultation, the patient is asked to choose four 'Balance' bottles with as little preconception as possible. The choice of bottles indicates the story of the person, the pattern from which they have evolved.

The first 'Balance' choice is the representation of the soul as far as the present consciousness of the person can perceive it. It shows the potential, the life purpose and the life lesson, the true aura.

The second bottle indicates problems that have had to be overcome and generally shows the process of evolvement.

The third bottle is the 'here and now' in relation to the potential of one's soul purpose.

The fourth bottle again shows the present situation but in relation to the energies moving towards us from the future.

The second and third choices generally relate to the physical and mental condition of the person. The fourth choice relates to the tendencies likely to arise. The fourth bottle should show one of the colours of the first bottle either in variation or subtlety. When there is no matching between the first and fourth bottle it can indicate a pocket of resistance. The last selection is the 'key' that opens the gate to the full knowledge and healing of the person. The key is that which correlates past with the present.

Having discussed the colour code or interpretation with the patient we will have unlocked some of the emotional and spiritual levels which the symbolism of the colours have unfolded.

At this juncture, the patient should shake the bottles fairly vigorously. It is then noted whether the bubbles are small and active and whether the activity remains full for at least a count of six before the two layers begin to separate again. If it does, it indicates good energy generally, unless the bubbles form a mass which would indicate a stagnation of energy, a 'pent-up' feeling.

What is happening is that the patient's energy fields are setting up minute waves of vibration within the oils of the bottle. These oils are highly sensitive, 'live' you could say, and reflect the state of the patient's field of vital force. A healthy person produces bubbles that readily settle – though not *too* readily – to re-form the two layers. An unhealthy person, or someone lacking in harmony, produces a cloudy effect that takes some time to clear.

If, after the onset, the bubbles that remain become large and rimmed, there is turmoil and turbulence present, a 'fasten your safety belt' situation. If you find this, you need peace, dear reader, and the all-blue 'Balance', the 'peace' bottle could provide it (see page 109).

Readings are taken on *three levels*.

The first level is the soul or spirit level.
(a) The first bottle represents the patient's aura and their true purpose and potential.
(b) The second bottle shows the progress of the soul through time – the mid-point in the evolution of the soul towards the present.
(c) The third bottle shows the present point in the soul's development towards its purpose.
(d) The fourth bottle indicates the energies from the future moving toward the fulfilment of the soul's potential.

The second level is the mental/emotional level.
(a) The first bottle now represents the subconscious in the base fraction and the conscious mind in the top fraction.
(b) The second bottle indicates the major emotional and mental problems that exist between what one came into the world with and what one is dealing with in the present.
(c) The third bottle shows the present emotional situation in the top fraction and the past emotional situation in the lower fraction.
(d) The fourth bottle pertains to the likely emotional/mental

outcome of the present situation and the energies moving toward the patient.

The third level is the physical level. Regard each of the bottles now as a body, the base fraction representing the lower torso and legs, the upper fraction representing the upper torso, arms and head. The second bottle is now taken by the patient in the left hand and held with the cap between the index and middle finger and the thumb underneath to support the bottle's weight. It is then well shaken to the count of six and handed back to the practitioner. This enables the vibrations of the patient to enter the fluids within the bottle thus feeding information to the practitioner via the bubbles, bows and striations. This, added to the causative factors already assimilated from the spiritual and mental/emotional levels enables the practitioner to interpret the physical situation.

Any of the four bottles may be shaken but the second is usually chosen as it indicates the causative factors leading to the present, and therefore shows more depth and insight than the third, which represents the present. The first shows physical conditions in early life and the fourth indicates physical tendencies in the future.

Thus there is a complete picture in the variations and combinations of the chosen bottles of that which is in you. Your 'inner tuition' must be your guide in the interpretation of it.

Let us return for a while to the fourth choice of bottle, which has been termed the 'key'. So many come for help, longing for release and healing, yet there is within them a secret place, a pocket of resistance that they will neither look at nor touch. It is within this sphere that the 'key' plays its most important part, for when the key can be turned, the holistic process of healing is set in motion. This usually brings in its wake the releasing therapy of tears. At such moments we can be sure healing has started.

On one of my visits to Denmark, I held a session with a circle of healers at the home of our hostess, Annemaria. She supplied small white candles for everyone. A lighted candle was placed in a holder and handed to me. I stood in the centre of the circle. One by one, silently, they came to light their small candles from mine and then resumed their places. The lights had been switched off and the circle around me was illuminated by the soft glow of the candles. One could almost hear the wings of the angels.

There were many there, some to heal and many to be healed. A dear lady in a wheel-chair also held a candle, and several children stood, their little faces literally aglow in the candlelight. Standing there in the midst I remembered suddenly the words, 'Suffer the little children to come unto me'. That day, a whole family was reunited in love, where before there had been bitterness and almost hate. Mother and daughter were weeping openly now in each other's arms. I kissed the tears upon their cheeks, sharing with them the healing. Tasting the salt upon my lips, I knew then why tears are salt. They are God's own cleanser from the heart, from the soul, the pure salt of remorse and re-awakened love bringing healing and restoration as they pour forth. The gateway to all healing is *dedication* and the key that opens the gate is *love*.

One of the ways 'Balance' can be used for finding out which part of a patient's body is sick is as follows. The practitioner takes the second choice of bottle and then shakes it at different points over the patient's body surface within the region of the aura. Information about the various organs beneath is obtained by observing whether the two layers are readily reformed or whether the oils tend to remain opaque.

The doctor who could diagnose but offer no remedy would be useless. Hence, the practitioner, having an accumulation of evidence and decided what is the problem, then uses the intuition that is latent in everyone and proceeds to advise, re-balance and heal holistically.

The treatment recommended to the patient is likely to include the absorbing of the vital colour energy from his or her own 'Balance' at regular intervals. It may be applied to the skin over the affected region (simply shake the bottle to mix the two colour fractions before rubbing on). The 'Balance' oils will show their therapeutic effects when the patient is gazing at them, or even merely being in their vicinity.

Looking at coloured cards, painted walls or any inanimate object won't do nearly so well. The colours must be *living* colours; the light carries the colour and that works upon the light within. They relate, wavelength upon wavelength.

The 'Balance' combinations usually used to treat specific ailments and conditions are detailed in the next two chapters.

To end this chapter, I'd like to tell you about something that happened to me, proving the energizing effect 'Balance' can have.

One Christmas I was feeling like death warmed up. The weather was bad, so I couldn't go on my usual walk. Instead, for exercise I had to use my static bike which is kept in the room in which the 'Balance' range of bottles is displayed. I was pedalling away like mad and feeling utterly exhausted. It then happened that I switched on the light. And do you know, my energies suddenly came back and I could pedal away again.

I thought, how funny! What has given me the energy? Then I realized. You fool! It's your own bottles! They're feeding back!

The Chakras

The human body has been likened to a busy little factory with its storehouses. The cells of our body are manufacturing units engaged in supplying the materials needed for harmony and health. They are also disposal units for waste and unwanted substances, acting as cleansing stations. The Creator has designed our body to be a self-renewing and self-healing unit. The parts, however, have to be maintained, like a car's, and if any one organ is overtaxed, the storehouse runs out of replenishing material and cannot cope with the overload. It is then that Aura-Soma colour therapy comes into the area of supply and demand. When the storehouse is depleted it must be 're-stored'.

However, Aura-Soma's work does not stop there, and even though we seek to satisfy those 'who must measure' we must also remember the spiritual and mental aspects, and that we are dealing with live energies.

Yoga and other Eastern teachings maintain that within the human body is a huge column of moving energy made up of three main channels, coursing from the top of the head to the base of the spine. Where the channels intersect, energy wheels or centres are formed; these are referred to as the chakras. The Sanskrit word 'chakra' literally means a wheel or circle. Think then of seven vital chakras, located just to the front of the spinal column. They are the very core of the aura, and in order to ensure that the energies flow in harmony, that the complete being – mind, body, spirit – is 'in tune', each chakra should be fully open and in balance. Aura-Soma's work begins here.

It's so simple it's simply amazing. It works on the same principle as tuning in to a wireless or television set. Each chakra governs a specific area of the body. By applying the appropriate colour, whose wavelength is the key to the chakra needing help, the weakened wavelength is reinforced. Thus we help set in motion the regenerative and healing processes within the body cells themselves. This is merely a matter of supply and demand, and a rebalancing of the body.

Well-being is being well balanced.

Colour	Chakra and physical area	Influences and effects
Violet	Crown/Top of Head	Anti-inflammatory, Spiritually calming.
Indigo	Brow/Pineal	Helps inspiration and intuition. Anti-inflammatory.
Blue	Throat/Base of Skull	Helps communication, physically and spiritually. Promotes peace. Anti-inflammatory.
Green	Heart/Lungs	Space-giver. Inbringer of harmony. Decision-maker. Effective for heart conditions, physical and emotional. Helps lung conditions.
Yellow	Solar Plexus/Stomach Liver/Gall-bladder Spleen	The wisdom ray. Strengthens hormonal and nervous systems. Helps digestive tract. Muscle relaxant.
Orange	Navel/Kidneys Abdomen/Lower Back	A shock absorber, past and present. Strengthens etheric body. Cleanses the aura. Helps under-active conditions within the abdomen.

Red	Base of Spine	For spiritual grounding.
	Reproductive organs	Imparts vitality.
		Stimulates under-active conditions, e.g. sluggish circulation, weakened muscles, bowel inactivity, impotence and frigidity.

Table 1 above and the Aura-Soma chakra chart on page 2 show the colours that are the key to the various chakras. However, in Aura-Soma 'Balance' therapy, it has been found that the most effective combinations are not usually the single colour oils but those in which a colour near to it in the sequence is part of the combination. For example, instead of all-red, gold-over-red is usually recommended. A 'Chakra Set' of 'Balance' bottles consists of the following:

Gold/red (base chakra)
Orange/orange (navel chakra)
Yellow/gold (solar plexus chakra)
Blue/green (heart chakra)
Blue/blue (throat chakra)
Blue/purple 'Rescue' (head chakra)
Blue/pink (child's 'Rescue' – a subtle version of blue/purple for protection against emotional trauma)

The all-red, and all-green bottles are sometimes the right choice in specific circumstances, and for certain people, and so are included in this chapter.

The wavelength of each colour of the spectrum has been determined by scientists. They have found, surprisingly, that the greatest energizer of all, red, has the slowest rate of vibration of all the colours.

Red is allied to the base chakra and the reproductive organs. It is earth-drawn energy. In the Bible, blood is referred to as the life of the person, which of course it is. Red is a basic colour connected with basic emotions: love – red roses; anger – seeing red; virility – these are all *drive* emotions. It is the 'get up and go' colour. It is most important to have a good supply of such energy in order to get things done. Red prevails in abundance with leaders in any sphere of life. I believe that some astrologers associate the colour with Mars and with Venus.

Faded energies are nearly always seen as a lack of red vibrations in the composition of the person and could indicate a lack of iron and certain trace elements.

Red is always recognized as a danger signal and denotes emergency. It is with this in mind I advocate the all-red combination of Aura-soma 'Balance' for immediate energy, applied to the feet only. On the spiritual level, red should always be used after yoga, meditation and healing sessions as a 'grounding' colour. Here I would like to quote again my dear father: 'Beware of becoming so heavenly, you end up no earthly use.' Earthing is essential for all who are lifting their vibrations, whatever the medium. In layman's language – keep your feet on the ground!

The all-red 'Balance' must be treated with great respect. We do not advocate its use above the waist. It can bring out love, but be careful as it may be just the physical kind; gold is often needed for balance.

Red/red is useful for the following conditions:

pernicious anaemia;
impotence;
chilblains;
cramped muscles;
lack of energy/warmth.

You will notice from the Aura-Soma chakra chart on page 2 that in the region of the genitals I have placed an area coloured pink within the red area. Red is related to passion. When passion is spent, compassion finds its way into the situation. Pink is the colour of unconditional love, which is what the world needs most – the plants, animals and mankind. The motto therefore is 'Think pink'. When we love unconditionally, all that is base will be transmuted into something far deeper, greater.

We find that pink has a very great importance in the healing process, and that it literally stems from the womb; it does excellent work on all womb troubles and women's complaints. In these days of freedom, men are able to show the duality of their nature and don't have to conform to a totally male image. Pink can represent the acknowledgement of this, that they are not all-male, but also 'womb-man'.

Violence abounds today through unexpressed frustrations, but pink can play an important part in counteracting this. A Swiss professor, who was at one of my seminars in Denmark, told me that a pink light would calm any aggression. Apparently, at St Quentin prison in the USA, when the men become aggressive and restless, huge pink arc lights are switched on, and in time they all calm down. I have recently heard that at Hull Prison in Humberside a cell was painted pink for experimental purposes. Prisoners noted for their violence were placed in this cell and within minutes had calmed down. Prison officers remarked on the fact that in one case a hardened inmate had actually apologised – unheard of! So successful was this experiment that we understand that other prisons are considering using the same method.

The gold-over-red combination is carefully balanced, giving wisdom with energy, tempering the sex drive and bringing in the quality of love. It, too, works when the 'get up and go' has 'got up and gone', a feeling so many people understand. This combination can be safely applied as far up as the waist. Incidentally, it helps with all under-active conditions such as constipation, impotence and sluggish circulation, by its stimulating action. We refer to this beautiful combination as the 'sunset' bottle.

An amusing incident occurred during one of the exhibitions regarding this particular oil. Explaining to a group its purpose and potential, I referred to its stimulating quality and the aphrodisiac effect of the special essence ylang-ylang which it contained. A man sidled up to me quietly.

'I'll have one of those', he said, thrusting money at me.

I handed him the bottle. At that moment his wife, who had been at the opposite stand, came up. Noting the bottle her husband was clutching and having heard only part of the previous explanation, she exclaimed sharply: 'You don't want that, Alf.'

Alf clutched the bottle determinedly. There ensued a small exchange of words. The wife turned to me. 'What did you say it did, dear?'

'Dear' answered with a smile: 'It gives virility.'

'Oh,' she said, looking relieved. 'It's all right, Alf, you can have it. I thought she said fertility.'

The bystanders laughed. Alf went a little pink, but walked off happily with his precious bottle.

The following was written by Aura-Soma therapist and dental surgeon Anne Cannock.

> Vicky said, 'Look in the bottle and let it tell you.' So I did.
> **Red/Gold Oil.** The 'sunrise' bottle. To earth with wisdom.
> This is the yellow-gold of spiritual wisdom brought into earth use. It is wisdom brought to bear at solar plexus level where body, mind and spirit come together to bring forth energy, life and power into the here and now.
>
> It is the 'sunrise' bottle of the New Age and the 'New You', rising in all your glory into the consciousness of your own being.
>
> A confidence bottle of powerful energy directed by inner wisdom. For the bringing out of hidden potential, letting the real you get out.
>
> As with the all-red combination, this oil is a regenerator, to bring energy in and also to bring love out, but not just in a physical way, as it is balanced by the gold.
>
> It is the 'I am' bottle, for someone who needs the energy and wisdom to find his or her true identity, and for the person who allows his conscious mind to dominate his 'inner tuition', that is intuition. It could be useful for someone needing the all-green oil or the blue 'peace' bottle.

I AM

> I am all that I am
> One with the Universal Mind
> One with the source of all life
> I am one with all life forms
> And they are one with me
> I am love, I am life, I am peace
>   ... I am.

The **gold-over-red** is good for dysfunctions and pains in the following areas:

feet;
legs;
reproductive organs;
bladder;
intestines;
any underactive part of the body.

It helps in the following conditions:
impotence;
painful menstruation;
under-active menstruation;
infertility;
constipation.

Another chakra combination is the all-orange. This has been described as relevant to gut reactions. It is the shock absorber of the system. Phobias and fears, such as agoraphobia, claustrophobia and deep psychological disturbances, stemming maybe from the deep recesses of memory, all respond to this lovely oil. The heart may well be affected by the phobia or shock, but it is in the gut that the reaction takes place on a purely physical level. The description of a brave man as having 'guts' simply has its origin in this.

Orange acts upon the adrenal area, so it is easy to see that after operations, severe accidents, nervous breakdowns or in any case of shock, this colour would be helpful. Sportsmen call upon this colour a great deal – their need for adrenalin is particularly high.

In application, all 'Balance' oils should be used in girdle fashion, completely around the body. Orange belongs to the area just above the reproductive organs and below the navel.

I have often referred to this colour from the spiritual angle as the 'Humpty Dumpty' bottle. On page 189, there is a reference to the etheric gapping that occurs in shock conditions. I have noted, time and time again, the movement of the 'true aura' to the periphery of the body, the slip-road provided by the etheric (the ether around the body), where the divine spark may rest until help and healing have taken place. Through this etheric gapping there can be energy loss. Often the layman refers to this unknowingly, saying that, since so and so happened, he has felt disorientated, and physically and mentally unable to 'get it together again' – truly a Humpty Dumpty situation.

> *Humpty Dumpty sat on a wall*
> *Humpty Dumpty had a great fall.*
> *All the king's horses and all the king's men*
> *Could not put Humpty together again.*

This condition can exist and continue through timelessness itself, with deep inner disturbances giving rise to physical manifestations and 'inexplicable' disorders. Many therapists have found that the orange combination used on the periphery of the body works well. It is always a great satisfaction when Humpty Dumpty gets it together again.

Orange/orange is very useful both before and after operations. It is also good for the following:

nervous depression;
suppressed fears;
etheric shock;
disorientation;
thyroid problems and other hormone imbalances;
accidents;
tense muscles;
aggression;
skin troubles;
digestive troubles.

We travel now a little higher, to the solar plexus chakra, the 'spaghetti junction' of the autonomic nervous system. Here the dual combination of yellow-over-gold comes into play. Being physically allied to this nerve centre as well as the digestive organs, it serves very well for so many of the stomach and digestive upsets which appear to have a stress or nervous origin, such as dyspepsia, anorexia nervosa and bulimia. It seems to reharmonize all the neighbouring digestive organs, helping them to function more efficiently.

Many skin ailments are of nervous origin and respond to the yellow-over-gold combination which we refer to as the 'sunlight' bottle.

From the mental point of view, the 'sunlight' bottle gives one a psychological lift. It brings a promise of spring, a newness of life, a new beginning – the sunlight we so badly need after the depletion of winter, during convalescence or nervous debility. There is an innate longing for sunlight and the restoring of the light energies in spring. People suddenly begin to emulate the white of light and the yellow and gold of the sun in their summer clothes.

One of the early feedbacks we received was from someone using the yellow/gold oil for digestive troubles. Delightedly she reported that not only had it helped with these, but she had noticed that her embarrassing post-menopausal flushes were considerably lessened. This and other evidence suggests that the yellow/gold oil is an effective hormonal rebalancer.

It is a powerful combination, dealing not only with digestive, skin and hormonal problems but with muscular disorders too. Its action as a muscle relaxant can be better understood when one thinks about the body's automatic reactions in nervousness and fear. There is a noticeable tensing of the musculature. Lips tighten, jaws clench, the whole body stiffens in an effort to control the nervousness within. Like primitive man, we are prepared for flight or fight. Shall we suppose that in the alleviation of the nervous tension the body can revert to its normal muscular tone. Physiotherapists find this particular oil excellent in general massage and particularly helpful for their chronic cases. Sportsmen like to use it as a muscle oil before and after their activities.

On the spiritual level, a diffusion of gold can sometimes be seen psychically around the 'true aura'. This denotes an old soul, one highly evolved, a spiritual leader, a teaching master. The ultimate in spiritual development has been depicted in religious art as a golden halo, which is simply the etheric echo of a completely golden aura. This same gold is present but diffused with blue when an 'auric flight' is in progress, an occurrence just before the passing of a soul into the continuity of life (see page 188).

Yellow/gold is of benefit in the following conditions:

indigestion;
flatulence;
nausea;
hiatus hernia;
diverticulitis;
diabetes;
menopausal flushes;
chronic rheumatism;
arthritis;
anorexia;
dyslexia;
phobias.

The heart chakra, adjacent to the solar plexus, is our next subject – the receiving centre, the emotional centre of the being. The specific advocated here is blue-over-green. Separately, the green is seen as pure emerald which, when shaken, becomes the beautiful green of Chinese jade. Green is nature's space-giver in which a soul may stretch. It is the polarizer and centralizer of the being, bringing awareness of the true need and thereby giving the capability of decision with action.

When the feeling of self-encapsulation occurs, one has the sensation of being trapped by circumstances and indecisions. In such a situation, my wise father would say: 'Go hug a tree. Find a wise old tree where the sap has settled and the branches are held out in everlasting benediction.' Green helps the need for space.

I have heard it said by the more materially-minded that green is also an inducer of material gain. I make no comment on that level but would agree that when one knows where and with whom one is going, what and who one is, recognizing the true Godhead within oneself, then the right signals are sent out and could attract what is needed.

Physically, the effect of blue/green on the heart chakra is one of calming and stretching, and I personally find this combination excellent for angina. A possible explanation could be in the fact that, as mentioned before, it is an opening out, a medium to relax cramping situations, a category into which angina could fit.

In the region of this chakra lie the lungs. Asthmatics and bronchitics also respond to the same relaxing principle. The inclusion of the blue in the combination has its own balancing purpose. Blue, of course, is directly related to the throat chakra and it is easy to recognize the emotional tie-up between the heart emotions and the throat reactions, often referred to as 'choked'. Residual coughs, too, seem to be helped by the decongestive properties of the blue/green.

Theories can always come under question when argued from the materialistic point of view, but there is one conclusive statement I like to refer to. It concerns the blind man who was repeatedly questioned after his healing as to the method employed. 'I don't know,' he said again and again. Then he remarked, 'But this I do know – once I was blind and now I can see.'

In affairs of the heart, blue/green seems to work very well, making space for the right emotions and granting peace within. Causal depression is benefited by this colour combination. (This must not be confused with nervous depression, which has its basis in fears rather than in facts and for which the yellow/gold combination works best.) Pending divorce, broken affairs, failure in work are usually the causes for such depression. Menopausal depression is brought about by the sudden awareness of a watershed in life, the realization that in the giving of self in the rearing of children and the care of elderly parents, no time has been devoted to developing one's own potential.

As I mentioned in chapter 14, I see a lot of blue and green in the auras of Atlanteans, likewise with sea birds, dolphins and other sea mammals. In land birds there is a great similarity, but here the blue becomes turquoise.

Let me tell you of an interesting observation I made several years ago during my 'stand and stare' time. The starlings had been chattering busily on the lawn. I noticed that a solitary one, like a silent sentinel, was outlined on a huge oak tree farther off. The first hint of winter was in the air. There was such excitement among the birds, hundreds of them, their blue/green auras sparkling. Wonderingly, I looked again at the bird on its own and saw that its aura was different. There was a golden streak through the centre. I saw no such streak in any of the others. As if at a signal, the flock flew straight to the huge tree, completely surrounding the bird I had noted. The boughs were heavy with them. The chattering intensified, being no doubt last-minute instructions to the young ones and an interchange of pleasantries. Then my lone bird was in the air, leading the circling mass, and they were off.

After this, I watched carefully, noting there was always one bird with a golden-streaked aura, and it was this bird which inevitably led the others. Sitting at our window recently, dictating this book to Ann Whithear, I became aware of several small, blue and green auras on the common. The plaintive cries announced seagulls, driven inland by storms and cold weather. I noted one with the golden streak. I commented on this to Ann, who was writing busily.

'That one will leave first and the others will follow,' I said.

Ann was immediately intrigued by what I had to say. 'Let's write it down,' she said, and so we have.

Let us now consider the throat chakra, to which the beautiful heavenly blue-over-blue, the 'peace' bottle is allied. We always refer to this as the 'peace that passes all understanding'. Visually, I regard it as one of the most powerful colours in our collection. In meditation, yoga, healing, or in any situation where spiritual 'lift-off' is anticipated, the vibrations emanating from this colour

Green/green is a centralizer, and aids decision-making. It gives space for the mind to travel. It is good for stabilizing the astral body, and helps to relieve tensions. It stimulates the pituitary gland and promotes muscle and tissue building, though it can also counteract overactive cell growth. Green helps the blood and circulation system. It also has an antiseptic action.

This combination is good for:

shock;
following operations, particularly for cancer patients;
fatigue;
combating malignant cells.

Blue-over-green is good for the following:

rash on chest;
heart symptoms;
midriff pain;
fibrositis;
asthma;
chronic bronchitis;
angina owing to over-exertion
epilepsy;
depression.

are in attunement with the Infinite.

Clairvoyants have described this colour as a means of contact and communication 'through the veil'. I quote here an incident related to me by a clairvoyant. She had purchased a chakra set of Aura-Soma 'Balance', placing the bottles in the sanctuary where she carried out her healing work. Among the collection, of course, was the heavenly blue. Shortly afterwards, I received a call to say that the blue had faded completely. Was this significant, as the other colours were not affected? She then told an astonishing story.

Her parents had been staying with her, and her mother had set out alone on a long train journey to visit her son. Some time after her mother's departure, the woman received a message from her brother to say that there had been an accident and her mother lay critically ill in hospital. Panic stricken, she dropped everything and she and her father rushed to the hospital. They arrived a fraction too late; her mother had travelled on. Her father was distraught and there was no consoling him. He was convinced that his wife had gone in turmoil and that there was no peace within her, especially since he had not been there. No doubt it was the shock of such an abrupt severance that coloured his feelings. Returning home did not lessen his despair, and his poor daughter, herself in shock, found it almost impossible to cope with him. After a few days, imagine her surprise when, upon returning home, she found her father seated in the sanctuary holding the all-blue bottle that was now completely colourless. From that moment, he became calm, almost as if he had received an inner reassurance.

In my opinion – and this I mentioned to my dear friend – her mother had sought this means of communication to console the bereaved and then reassure that peace now prevailed. The blue 'Balance', of course, is known as the 'peace' bottle. Since then, I have heard of many such incidents.

The blue, I feel, is a link between heaven and earth, and it has long been acknowledged as a spiritual colour. It is used on altars in churches, and I think it is no idle chance that artists through the ages have painted the Holy Mother Mary attired in heavenly blue. Incidentally, it was also the colour of King David and his shield. This thread of colour not only weaves its way through spiritual history but through life itself, from conception to the journey into the Greater Garden.

It is amazing how a pregnant woman reaches out subconsciously for blue and appears to be 'tuned in' at this level, for conception of itself must be grounded in red for the life energies needed, and the instinctive upreach to the spiritual blue brings this earth body into absolute balance with the spiritual soul that it is about to inhabit. Does this, then, tend to explain the affinity of this same blue for the infant itself?

The blue light that is now used in hospitals to heal jaundiced babies is but one instance. Gentle and soothing, it is a lovely colour for children when teething or infection upsets them. It is also for all the ailments that seem to occur with little ones – the measles, sneezles and tweezles that manifest themselves just as you are setting off on holiday!

Visually, blue has a great effect in the nursery where nightmares sometimes occur. Often these are just a flashback in time, old karmas and experiences relived momentarily. They can affect children very deeply, especially the slightly older child who cannot bring himself to speak of these things. Bed-wetting may well be a sign of inner disturbance. Most definitely peace and protection are needed in the room where the child sleeps. Again, I toss a thought into your lap – the need for light with children in such circumstances. They are afraid of the darkness. But, in fact, there is no such thing as darkness, merely lack of light.

Those niggling sore throats that occur and recur without warning, emotionally induced or otherwise, respond very well to the blue 'Balance'.

Physically, it relates to the thyroid and the thymus, which are endocrine glands. The thyroid is the thermostat of the body, controlling the rate of metabolism. When this balance is disturbed and the thermostat setting is increased, the calming effect of blue acts to rebalance.

And now the last, but not the least, member of the 'Chakra Set', the blue-over-purple, the beautiful Aura-Soma 'Rescue'. This is allied to the top chakra, corresponding with the crown of the head, the brain and pineal gland. 'Rescue' is a spiritual and physical healer of great potency and its functions are many and miraculous.

This particular oil contains four of the most powerful chakra colours embodying both ends of the spectrum, violet and blue, magenta and red, which, when shaken, amalgamate to form a beautiful indigo. It is ranked by some as 'top of the pops'. As well as its mental and spiritual aspects, the 'Rescue' resonates with

Blue/blue is useful for businessmen under stress, and for anxious, expectant fathers. It also helps in the following conditions:

pregnancy;
children's ailments;
teething;
bruises;
infections;
over-active thyroid;
vocal problems.

all the chakras. On a higher level, it forms the connection of earth to heaven and heaven to earth, for a little red is incorporated, as is seen when light is shone through the bottle.

'Rescue' is known as the healer's bottle, and many have remarked upon its ability to open the 'third eye', giving psychic perception. There are those who use it for anointing, no doubt following the biblical injunction, 'Anoint thyself with oil'. This age-old custom has its deeper healing and spiritual meaning. It is the taking into oneself of the physical and spiritual help that is so necessary for a person to function fully, to become a rounded, whole being. The 'Rescue' is the most sensitive and the highest spiritual oil. Its full power can be felt in meditation and the sense of depth and understanding which it seems to impart is known to many. It is the most mystical, most exciting combination of all, and the most practical; it is an outreaching into space, a down-pulling for constructive thought and an aid to perceptiveness.

The blue/violet is a wonderful polarizer for the psyche. Applied to the occipital area, the psychic door at the base of the skull adjoining the spine, it rebalances, restores and rescues the psyche. Amnesia and inability to concentrate respond well to the 'Rescue'. Incidentally, it is a favourite with regression therapists because of its ability to free thought. The living energies held within this oil are a never-ending source of discovery.

This 'Balance' is literally a key, opening the doors to all the chakras. Used alone or in conjunction with the relevant chakra colour, it is nature's natural painkiller. Many find it an absolute essential in the kitchen, bathroom and car, for when applied immediately it acts as an instant first aid in all kinds of emergency. Bruises, burns, scalds, all manner of pain, even tooth extraction, seem to respond to the 'Rescue'. It can be reapplied at frequent intervals until the pain or swelling subsides. It is indeed an angel of mercy. In fact, I feel like quoting the famous Hoover advertisement, 'Every home should have one'.

We have had considerable feedback from people who have used the 'Rescue', telling of its help with tumours, cysts, warts and even the scourge of the swimming pools, verrucae. It can be used wherever the growth of cells has become overactive, and I record here one such episode.

For the fourth time one morning my doorbell rang. I was in the midst of meditation and did not welcome interruption. I knew that Phyllis, my faithful former housekeeper, would answer the door and hoped she could deal with the caller. My hopes were shattered. Phyllis tapped on the garden room window.

'Sorry', she said quietly, 'but the lady said she had come a long way, and it's urgent. She needs to talk to you.'

The word 'need' must always be heeded. I 'earthed' thoroughly and then went to greet her. She seemed very excited. The aura I was beholding was lovely and the predominance of blue told me that in spite of the excitement, there was a peace within her.

'You won't know me. My name is Mrs H', she said. I smiled inwardly, for I had just looked through the windows of her soul. True, I did not know her name, nevertheless, we were not strangers.

'I just had to come and tell you. I bought one of your oils from Marie Louise [Marie Louise Lacy, a well-known counsellor and lecturer in colour, and one very dear to my heart] specifically for my varicose veins. It's the blue and violet oil, the one you call the "Rescue". I had heard it was good for varicose veins. Well, the oil was miraculous!'

I listened carefully. She continued, 'My varicose veins are a little better.'

At this I wondered, where then, did the miracle lie.

'I'm sorry, dear, that you didn't get your miracle.'

She laughed excitedly. 'But I did, I did!'

This contradiction puzzled me. But as she went on, words tumbling over themselves, I began to understand. It seemed she had recently had a scan for a growth on her neck, in the thyroid region. It had grown unsightly and was becoming an embarrassment to her. The test had shown the growth to be benign, but the 'we will keep a watch on it' from the hospital did nothing for her peace of mind. Nor did the information that, because of its position on the thyroid, the growth should not be removed at this stage and that medication was not available either. The sword of Damocles hung over her head.

'I was fed up, I can tell you,' she said. 'It was ugly and worrying, and I found it all very unsatisfactory. I put the oil on my legs that night – I'd been using it for about two weeks – and there was still some left on my hands. I thought idly that I'd use it up on my neck, just to clear my hands. It felt good, so I continued for the next three nights, putting it on my legs and then on my throat. But by the fourth night my throat had come up in an angry red rash! My husband was alarmed and told me to stop using the oil immediately. He said I was obviously allergic to it. It didn't occur to either of us that I had been applying the oil for a fortnight to my legs without ill effect. Anyway, the rash gradually subsided, and three days later I put my hands up to feel if it had gone completely. It had – and so had the growth!'

The rash was what we call a 'healing crisis'. It often occurs when there is something very toxic to overcome. That was two years ago. There has been no return, and the lady in question has since attended one of my workshops.

The red and gold/red at the one end of the spectrum, relating to the base chakra, as I have said, acts on under-active conditions. At the other end of the spectrum and of the chakra range, the blue/purple deals with over-active conditions. Think of them, then, as opposite ends of the spectrum but working side by side, creating perfect holistic balance. It may be of help in memorizing the facts if I give 'for instances': gold/red to treat constipation, blue/purple for diarrhoea; gold/red for renal retention, blue/purple for cystitis; gold/red for sluggish circulation, blue/purple for hypertension (high blood pressure); gold/red for under-active thyroid, the 'Rescue' for over-active thyroid.

The great value is that both oils can be used conjointly. For example, if one needed energy, better memory and mental stimulation, the gold/red used on the feet or palms of the hand would be right to bring in mental and physical stimulation. But so that the mind might not become over-active, the blue/violet placed on the top chakra would bring calmness and aid assimilation.

The blue/violet/magenta oil, the 'Rescue', has many faces, many facets. Within this combination lies an abundance of the unseen colours of the Greater Garden. Maybe you know about the poet Goethe's 'unseen colour' – he could see a colour that others couldn't. I too can see this colour, and others that I cannot explain. The 'Rescue' bottle holds this unseen colour. I cannot tell you what it is, but it envelops every earthly colour and an unseen colour. It is the colour of the whole rainbow spectrum all in one – both ends. That is as near as I can go to describing it. We need not be surprised, therefore, that 'Rescue' can act on *all* areas of the body, wherever there is disharmony or pain.

The beloved 'Rescue' is one I use constantly because of its special powers, as a demonstration through which the true potential of the person can be revealed.

Sitting before me in desolation and despair is a rather colourless woman, with an uncaring and uncared for look about her. The signals she is sending out are very weak, and yet, as I regard her, the personal or 'true' aura, although paled almost to the point of insignificance, lights up in my consciousness. I detach. In the flashback of time, I see the glowing, beautiful soul (or aura) clearly revealed and shining through. What a powerful potential! I look straight into her eyes, the windows of her soul, and roll back the curtains. Here before me is no drab aura but the one whose journey through the soul's spiral has been of great worth. But the 'evolvement' has ceased and been nullified in this life – she is her own executioner. Striving to become socially acceptable, rather than spiritually aware, she has created her own blockage. The signals that she sends are basic earth level, and that is exactly what she is attracting. The desire within me grows to free the blockage within this woman, for here I recognize an important labourer in the harvest of the New Age.

Her voice reaches me once more. 'I'm a disaster area. Everything I touch goes wrong.'

I look at her with love. My hand reaches for the 'Rescue'. I place it before her. 'That,' I say, 'represents you, as you are and as the world sees you and as you have begun to see yourself, out of love with yourself. But you know the times when the world is silent around you, and deep calls unto deep, that this is not the true self. Now,' – and this time I smile – 'let me show you, dear girl, the potential, the possibilities, the true you!'

I lift the bottle, and in my other hand I hold my torch, the light I use to release the energies within the colours. I point once more to the bottle.

'This is how the world sees you when it has not time to stand and stare. But' – and now I shine the light through the base of the bottle – 'when the light of love, of self-understanding, and the love of another is shone through you, this is what is revealed.'

The colour has changed into a breathtakingly beautiful purple/magenta, glowing deeply with a hint of red and the faint reflection of blue. I see once more her aura, and now the oil is but a reflection of that within her. The eyes brim over with tears.

'Look at yourself,' I say. 'Look at your true self. Are you not beautiful? Can you see the power and potential within you, the real you? Know yourself, and then to yourself be true.'

The scales have dropped from her eyes, she is now weeping unashamedly. I hand her a paper tissue (a stock of which I have learned to keep readily available).

'Now,' I say, 'go out and do the work for which you are truly destined. Stop seeking from others and learn to serve. You will suddenly find that the signals you are sending out will alter and, as you learn to love yourself as you truly are, you will no longer project upon others your own inabilities and failures, and thus you will be able to love your neighbour as yourself. In this way you will learn that love is always being recycled.'

Blue/purple 'Rescue' alleviates the following conditions:

poor memory;
burns;
bruises and contusions;
infections (especially sore throats);
neuralgia;
insomnia;
headaches;
high blood pressure;
sinus congestion;
acute bronchitis;
acute cystitis;
diarrhoea;
lumbago and sciatica.

In an emergency, if the 'Rescue' does not immediately relieve the pain then an additional application of the personal aura colour (the first one chosen) should be applied to reinforce it. Alternatively, the actual chakra colour which is attuned with the appropriate herbs and essences for the area could also be used. Evidence shows that these, as in aromatherapy, enter into the body via the lymphatic system.

To conclude, I will describe how the chakras can be balanced using the Aura-Soma 'Colorcurium'. This lovely form of home treatment is available to all. It is used somewhat like a solarium or sun-lamp. The 'Chakra Set' of 'Balance' bottles stand on glass shelves, in order of the chakra sequence, with gold/red at the bottom and blue/violet at the top. A light is directed on the bottles, either from above or below. These then act as a power-station, re-energizing, regenerating, allowing the chakras to rebalance themselves. The life energies are thus able to flow, without any blocking.

You can stand or, if you like, sit down and read, in front of the 'Colorcurium'. There is no time limit for the treatment. You cannot burn yourself. You need at least 20 minutes for maximum benefit.

Now supposing, for example, I have some indigestion one day. The chakra bottle relating to the stomach is the yellow/gold one, so I move it to the top shelf alongside the blue/violet one and give myself the treatment. If my heart is a bit tired, I would bring the blue/green bottle up, and so on. Whatever is troubling you, simply adjust the chakra bottles as described.

There is an exceptional circumstance in which other 'Balance' combinations apart from those in the 'Chakra Set' may be used in the 'Colorcurium'. This occurs when the second and third choices of 'Balance' bottles do not include any of the 'Chakra Set' combinations. In this instance the aura colour should be used instead. For example, somebody might pick the all-green 'Balance' as his second or third choice, so this would be substituted for the blue/green chakra colour.

Subtleties of Aura-Soma 'Balance'

The 'true aura', the soul, the higher consciousness, that which continues on its spiral journey from the beginning to eternity, contains its own personal record and, as fingerprints can identify a person, so this aura can identify the soul essence. Everything experienced from the beginning of time has left its mark upon this personal aura, which should not be confused with the physical aura. The latter is an electro-magnetic field whose colours relate to chakras, the energy wheels that determine bodily harmony and health. The 'true aura' looks, to those who can see it, like an egg-shaped core. It is also like a map, a record of the real personality, which imparts the complete soul sense and enables recognition of one for another. It is through aura recognition that an old soul recognizes those with whom he or she has travelled. Thus, twin souls meet and are knit together instantly – soul meets soul-mate.

The aura can appear faded, fragmented and sometimes cratered like the moon, but the true essence of the being never fundamentally alters. However, moods, matters of the moment and experiences are clearly displayed around the core of the aura and radiate on its periphery. It is interesting, sometimes disconcerting, to be conversing with a friend or acquaintance with a bland or smiling face, suddenly to see a darkening around the periphery of the core of the being. A friend of mine had a very good expression for this: 'They talk you fair but they think you foul.'

These moods, of course, are of the moment. But more important, and bearing upon the aura, is what one does to retard spiritual development. The betrayal of self literally colours (or perhaps I should say discolours) one's life. Anything that impedes the progress of self leaves its scar and creates a sick aura. This is nearly always the root cause of sickness which, physically, mentally and spiritually, is the outward manifestation of inner auric disturbance. It is essential that the aura be known and treated first. The release of the healing powers within oneself depends upon this particular cleansing process.

It is imperative that the therapist should remember to treat the sick aura before doing anything else – treating the symptom may alleviate the immediate problem but does not remove the underlying cause. Once the aura is being treated through direct application of the auric oil, the inducement of the flow within the chakras themselves can commence. Only then can the chakra treatment begin, using the appropriate wavelength of colour.

The 'Balance' bottles relating to each of the chakras, and the physical, mental and spiritual conditions that they alleviate, have been dealt with in the previous chapter. There are many subtle combinations of those already described, and this chapter is devoted to them. A complete list of the Aura-Soma 'Balance' range is to be found on page 199.

Yellow-over-green

The subtlety and symbolism within the yellow/green combination relates to the beginning of spiritual progress for the soul. The soul is seeking for its right space and place, represented by the green, within which to use wisdom, depicted by the yellow or gold. Green is the space, the freedom of the soul, for the soul must always be free. The spirit can and must go 'walk-about'. To restrict the soul brings only heart cramp and retards the progress. The soul has wings; it must fly where it will. The wisdom (yellow) is the channelling of this free soul, which uses its freedom for the purpose of its calling. The primary duty of everyone is to the essence of the higher consciousness.

Physically and mentally, the yellow (solar plexus) and the green (heart chakra) create harmony and well-being. This combination helps relieve confined, cramped and claustrophobic conditions, whether they be soul cramp or physical or mental states. It acts, too, by contrast, on agoraphobia. It brings decision where there is indecision and the wisdom, clarity of thought and calmness to go forward with courage. The yellow-over-green combination is an excellent 'make your mind up' oil, and suitable for any situation where one's rightful place seems threatened. Not only is it a good detoxifier, but it is useful for anxiety, for activating the thymus, strengthening bones, as a laxative and as a cerebral stimulant.

Green-over-gold

The green-over-gold combination represents the decision and the wisdom to choose rightly, bringing in the material and the spiritual, both of which are necessary to the progress of the individual. But even the wisest and the most golden of souls (the angels themselves have fallen, as in the case of Lucifer) may momentarily lose direction and space. The true soul self may then lie dormant, unexpressed, resulting in self-encapsulation. Imprisonment – physical, mental or spiritual – is the thief of time and calls for help and release. The green in the top fraction is the key that opens the prison door that the pure gold of being (bottom fraction) may go forth once more. There are many aspects and applications of this particular combination; it can help one climb back into life after physical or emotional trauma, and it is a very beneficial colour combination within which to meditate.

I have discovered through a painful, personal experience yet another, even deeper aspect of its healing purpose. This I pass on only to help others better to understand themselves and what is happening to them. The 'why', as yet, I cannot fathom, but that it has an explanation beyond even that which is revealed I am quite certain.

At the end of a beautiful workshop an over-enthusiastic student, hugging and lifting me in a boa constrictor squeeze of love, cracked three ribs. I was soon in acute pain. But it taught me a lesson, and I am grateful rather than resentful. My condition led to other repercussions. An unfortunate choice of pain killer was administered to me by an allopathic doctor and I found myself consigned to a geriatric ward. Blind, in considerable pain, I was left to my own devices. I cannot and will not give full details of the humiliation and degradation that took place within me. Suffice it to say, I felt my soul was being crucified.

Upon my return home, the pain, untreated, still persisted. Desperately the Aura-Soma 'Rescue', nature's own painkiller, was applied. To my surprise, for it had always acted before, there was only a minor response. It is a fact that one can be too close to a situation to solve it. There is an old saying, 'Every teacher needs a teacher.' One could also say, 'Every healer needs a healer.' To heal oneself or one's loved ones is always difficult, for if one is within soul touch, then panic can confuse one as to the real need. Phyllis, my ever-faithful friend, and very much a simple soul of the earth, overheard one of the therapists who was visiting me remark on the healing of an ill-treated horse by the use of the Humpty Dumpty oil, the all-orange. Phyllis had been with me for well over 40 years and was very much aware of the deep searing of the soul, and the fragmentation of the aura that had taken place. Suddenly she said, 'What about me using the orange oil for you?'

I looked at her, astonished, knowing full well the trauma that had occurred. Why hadn't I thought of this?

We applied it. On two levels, everything began to heal – Humpty Dumpty was getting it together again. The third level, however, the spiritual, still remained shattered. The needle had stuck on the record of time, and I was once more thrown back into all the ancient traumas and karmas of the past. I felt the loss of soul direction. It truly was a situation of 'Others He saves, Himself He could not save.'

This time it was Mike, who had been watching me with care and concern, who made a suggestion: 'Why not use the green-over-gold oil?' He had not read my interpretation of this colour combination, for the handbook in which it appears had not yet been published.* I used the green and gold combination and, at last, my body, mind and spirit resumed their onward journey. I

* *Aura-Soma Colour Notes: Advanced 1*

hope this serves in some way as a guide and direction. If so, then it will all have been worth while.

Yellow-over-blue

We return to green, the yin and yang, the coming together of yellow and blue. The soul in its hunger can find repast here. It is the upreaching, the striving of the soul, the feeling of wanting to rise above earthly matters, trying to bring into perfect balance the demands within oneself. This combination helps one find out who one is and what one is. One can wander in the labyrinth of the mind in safety.

The young may feel the need for this combination when the first stirring within themselves creates demand without the wisdom, as yet, to cope with it. This, perhaps, is the means of helping them to receive a balancing of the physical and spiritual. At this stage of the life when the young person is extremely vulnerable, and sensitive, there is a need to come to a full realization of his or her true mission and potential. Otherwise, there is a danger of living for the time and forgetting timelessness.

On a physical and emotional level, this oil may help restore balance in cases of neuroses, give direction to those in unsettled or unhappy circumstances and provide relief to sufferers from nervous dyspepsia, menopausal problems and stammering.

Turquoise-over-green

> *Like awakening spring*
> *This colour unfolds*
> *The gentle splendour*
> *Of life.*

> *Like the leaves in renewal*
> *The cycle of growth*
> *The unfolding of Spirit*
> *Into whole Truth.*

Far-seeing and being,
The vibrations are given,
Transformation beginning
Echoing, re-tuning
The colours transmuting
Into the One.

Stephanie Stevenson

I should like to tell you about the birth of this particular oil. It was conceived during a meditation in which I saw the soul spread itself as if with wings, making an upward and outward journey into heaven itself. The sheer beauty of this captured me as I became part of it. My inner being knew the meaning, and it was with joy that I found this corroborated the very next day when conducting a teaching session with one of my experienced therapists.

The turquoise/green oil stood on the consulting room table, ethereal in aspect, next to the intense blue/green combination of the heart chakra oil. There was a particular quality, a significance, about this new combination and vibrations of a totally different nature were emanating from it. The therapist's eyes seemed unable to leave it. Of the 31 combinations of oils standing there, this one alone was calling her. I smiled inside, for I knew what was happening.

'Strange', she said, 'I've always been attracted to and loved the strong blue/green oil. But for some reason I don't want to look at it any more. It seems to be part of the past, not satisfying the need within the present.'

Now I smiled openly. The upsurge of the spiritual had begun in her. It was not discarding the physical or the mental as represented by the blue/green combination, but rather through the communication of the soul the physical and mental were now being directed, in complete harmony, into their true programme. I said: 'This is a precious, magical moment. Hug it and hold it to yourself.' These treasured moments, sacred within themselves but all too swift in passing, are well known to all – the lover recognizing the beloved, the mother cherishing the child, the healer witnessing the first healing, the clairvoyant the first sighting. It is the beginning and the promise of fulfilment.

Blue and green together make turquoise, which represents the mind and body in its soul form balanced in harmony with the heavenly blue as depicted in the 'peace' bottle. Here is no indication of the turmoil of growth when it is purely physical, but rather the peace that comes with the realization of the higher self. This will have its bearing too on the sensitive or artistic child or teenager who although seeking the physical and mental levels is yet aware of the higher consciousness. They are on a soul search.

The dark blue/green combination of the heart chakra, as mentioned before, the 'big guns' as it were, should always be used in a physical or mental emergency – depression, epilepsy, angina due to over-exertion, chronic bronchitis, asthma, fibro-sitis and trauma in affairs of the heart. The turquoise/green oil should be used after these emergencies have been controlled, as a prophylactic preventing subsequent scarring of the soul.

Royal blue-over-turquoise

The turquoise is a colour related to the visionary, the woodland inhabitant, the forest, sea and sky. This combination is a lovely auric choice denoting the gentle wanderer on the face of the earth who nevertheless touches heaven with outstretched fingertips. Any external hardness is but a facade, a defence mechanism. Here is a person who relates to the animal and plant kingdoms but finds it very hard to relate to the human kingdom. This is a person who needs love, expects love, but considers it a weakness to show love, the dreamer with locked-in dreams who awaits the growing and completing time when the dreams can be recognized as realities, a being who better relates to the one person in all the kingdoms who can unlock unconditional love. But with the deepening of life with all its experiences (royal blue) comes the true dawning of self and soul consciousness, the release of locked-up emotions, the true potential emerging on its highest yet most practical level.

On the second level, the mental level, there is a need for concentration and application. This is a person of great capabilities whose mental energy is excellent but whose concentration has to be almost compulsory. Any form of authority may be resented. The mind has to accept that it is a means to its end, and meaningless gestures have no value. But here is a person who could be absolutely devoted to the one who turns the key.

Physically, it relates to a person very much controlled through the thyroid and pituitary glands, vulnerable to eye and throat infections. There should always be protective measures taken around the throat and head chakras, to which, of course, this oil relates especially. It may be a very effective combination for the heart, too, to help bring depth into any emotion or, incidentally, to create a depth in the would-be partner's emotion.

Spiritually, it represents a soul who is not yet aware of the strength and longing that lies within. When the true mirror of self is held before the being, or even perhaps when it is shown through the reflection of another, then the miracle happens. These are lovely people, both a surprise and a deep delight.

Royal blue-over-gold

The royal blue and gold combination brings in all past knowledge and ancient wisdoms, and relates particularly to the Inca and the Aztec peoples. It creates peace and wisdom within meditation, thus aiding the clairvoyant. When combined – the perfect balance of yin and yang – it will give space to the time-traveller (a person who travels 'out of the body' to places distant in time and space), for it is allied to inter-planetary travel. Space healers (those who cleanse the space around places with a bad atmosphere) will also relate to this. It is indeed a powerful, peaceful and purposeful combination. The royal blue, bordering on indigo, seeming to contain a subtle quality, is allied to religious symbolism, the kingships, Mother Mary, David, Solomon (it was the aura colour of Solomon, noted for his wisdom and chosen by spiritual selection).

From the mental aspect, this oil is excellent during examinations or at times of extra demands on the mind, bringing in wisdom and clarity of thinking. It is a teacher's bottle, useful for lecturers, speakers, those who marry pen to paper, and for anyone who has to impart knowledge. The royal blue harmonizing with the throat chakra helps impart power and eloquence in communication. This combination is good for stress, particularly where one feels trapped within a circumstance or place, as it brings decision, clarity of mind and wisdom to choose well.

Physically, the royal-blue-over-gold combination aids the heart and lungs and is admirable as an 'unblocker' for the solar plexus. In fact, it can be applied to any part of the body where blocking occurs. The thyroid and thymus are controlled and helped most by this deep blue colour. Sore throats respond well to this oil. But in the case of recurring throat troubles, the Aura-Soma 'Rescue', the blue-over-purple combination, should be brought in for reinforcement. The royal blue and gold oil is a good physical healer and balancer, and is advocated as a second application in conjunction with any other colour combination. Not only is this oil physically therapeutic, it is also spiritually protective. Spiritually, the blue, 'the peace that passeth all understanding', inexplicably calming with its complete attunement to the heavens themselves, brings communication on the highest spiritual level. However, the royal blue with its intense depth reaches out into the ethereal worlds, the worlds beyond. Those who choose instinctively this royal blue colour, be it over red, gold or green, betray an affinity with space and space dwellers and are usually concerned with other-world aspects – astrologers, lovers of the skies and the stars. In fact, the term 'spaced-out' could well apply here, but in a different sense. These are the very wise, yet admittedly different, including the so-called absent-minded professor or the person with no apparent regard for time, exasperating to the earth dweller, perhaps, but of great value to those who exist beyond this time.

Violet-over-violet

This violet-upon-violet oil is allied to the spirit itself and to a life of dedication. In other words, it relates to all who are wholly committed in the service of the true spirit, the healers of the

New Age world. It is the joining of soul to soul, violet upon violet, finding kindred spirits, the true violet of the East and of the West lying one upon the other. Thus shall we obtain the love and peace that passeth all understanding.

All spiritual leaders can be identified by their auras – violet with the golden periphery glowing and growing, which eventually will be seen as an emanation rising above the head, depicted and seen as a halo. These special people carry their own protection, for they have already laid down their lives for the service of others, eliminating the personal ego. But those of us not quite so evolved spiritually have great need of protection. This precious oil, creating the barrier to darkness that always seeks to destroy the light, brings protection to those as yet unable to fend for themselves completely. Violet is the colour that brings healing to the soul. Take this into your meditation, feel it swirling and enveloping every part of your being, physical, mental and spiritual. See it spiralling upwards, touching the very essence of your being. Know it within your mind, hold it against your heart, fold the wings of your spirit around it, stay gently resting upon it. Go where the spirit takes you and know yourself above the earth in touch with infinity and yet on earth.

In meditation it is essential that the descent back should be gentle, a sinking back through all the colours of the spectrum. Visualize each one as you descend – violet, indigo, blue, turquoise, green and gold. Stay a moment, breathe deeply, bid gentle and loving farewell, then pass deeper into orange, let everything fall quietly into place, slowly, without shock, touch the harmony within your whole being and there sink your feet into the earth. Let the red with its live and fiery energies engulf you, drawing you earthwards that it may be used on earth even as it is in heaven.

The child's soul, still vulnerable although held firmly by the silver cord, faces an earthly reality without the full armour of wisdom. In today's atmosphere, with its threats and hidden dangers, children, creatures of heaven, for of such is the kingdom of heaven, and of such is the New Age kingdom, need love and protection. Anoint them with oil, literally, that there may be a barrier between them and the dangers from without, and from within.

The New Age child, with his greater inner knowledge, perception and awareness, sees much more than the average child and, because of his higher vibrations, reacts instantly. He has extra need of prayer and protection and must be held perpetually in a constant circle of love. The mother and father of these special children should, in mind, thought and prayer, see them encircled and held safely within the sphere of the highest consciousness where only love can live and evil has no place or power.

This violet oil has a more gentle healing effect on the physical body than the Aura-Soma 'Rescue', the blue-over-purple oil. Its nature is one of preventative protection, calming all aggression in and around the body. It can be used as a protection for children before going to school, and may be helpful in cases of neuralgia, bruising, shock, pain and inflammation.

Green-over-violet

The choice of this oil is the sign of the being suddenly becoming aware of the still small voice, crying softly when all the world is quiet around: 'And what about me?'

It is the striving of the soul to find its true self, the space within which it can spread and breathe, and have its being. Life with its pressures and demands has drained the true colour from the being, but this is a time of realization; when the body is depleted or defeated the soul flies free and goes on.

I love it when I see a person pick up this bottle. For this is the soul who was lost and has now found itself. The soul is seeking a space in which it may stretch and grow, breathe once more so that the true potential and purpose for which it was programmed from the beginning may be released.

The green jewel fraction brings the ability to centralize and make the right decision, bearing harmony and purpose to the spiritual violet that lies beneath, waiting.

The word 'disease' is only a clinical term and one to which somehow I can never relate. It is merely a term describing symptoms, the 'dis-ease', or disharmony, within the entire person. One should not acknowledge the existence of irreversible illness, but rather recognize the power of positive thinking which can reverse 'dis-ease'.

The green-over-violet oil, producing a dark shade of jade when shaken, is useful for psychosomatic pain and illness, and for manic depressives.

Yellow-over-violet

Idealism must of necessity travel through the phase of realism to affect the fullness of 'evolvement'. The choice of the yellow-over-violet oil indicates a great spiritual guide. This is the person who 'came in' with the violet-over-violet range, then had to go through the red and the violet relating to earth and heaven, suffering to gain knowledge of healing, and then went onward to the rose-over-pink oil, bringing the experience of unconditional love into the New Age and love of true self through which one can love others. The yellow/violet combination is the ultimate plea for wisdom like Solomon's, to use the healing powers discerningly.

On the second level, the mental level, this combination is a good balancer if the mind is dominating the true essence, the violet, the healing within the person. This is almost a 'physician heal thyself' situation for the mind that has to measure. Many blocks can exist on all levels, spiritual, mental and physical. On the spiritual level, it can be caused through past karma or karmic memory. A person may be unable to pay the price of the knowledge he seeks. The solar plexus, the 'Spaghetti Junction' of the spirit, body and mind, is often the site of such blockage. This situation can be effectively dealt with by the release mechanism in the yellow/violet oil. Fears are resolved and take their true part in life as growth experiences, and the golden light begins to shine through once more. Unaccountable fears and phobias such as claustrophobia, agoraphobia and persecution complexes, are often caused by memories of bad experiences, perhaps in past lives, just penetrating the consciousness. This is the oil to use, for it will help to cast off such memories.

Physically, the yellow deals with the endocrine and nervous systems, with the violet bringing in the healing aspect. The symptoms of multiple sclerosis and Parkinson's disease may be greatly reduced by the use of the yellow-over-violet oil. The value of the pink oil in these circumstances must not be over-looked, for the situation brings with it a loss of self love. The person is literally out of love with the body that has, in his mind, let him down. It is an aggression trapped inside the being, as it were within the capsule of an unwilling body. So much love is needed here, not only by the person for him or herself, but also unconditional love from others.

Pink-over-violet

This oil represents the predestined healer who, since the beginning of his or her spiral growth, through karmic experiences in many reincarnations, has now learnt healing with unconditional love. This is a soul-stirring combination. When the base colour chosen is violet in any combination, then absolute single-mindedness exists. Nuns, monks and saints, all of whom are on a purely spiritual path, have to learn the lesson of relating to life in order that their mission of love and healing may be complete. These are truly advanced persons who have had to travel the path of spiritual development, have suffered and known all the tribulations of human life and now want to take up their full mission of healing, peace and unconditional love. Of these souls it is truly said: 'The harvest is plentiful but the labourers are few.' The choice of this bottle is an indication of one who has learned by karmic experiences and many reincarnations a lesson of unconditional love (pink fraction). All of us engaged in the 're-new-al' age need the pink-over-violet combination, for without love there can be no complete healing of this age.

On the mental level, the pink-over-violet oil can indicate one who requires love as well as one who gives it. This oil also acts to protect a spiritual person against aggression.

Physically, it relates to the top chakra, but it can also be used on any part of the body that requires healing. Love, the pink, can travel anywhere.

Violet-over-pink

Where there is an 'upside down' version of a combination, a reversal as it were, one might conclude that literally the life needs a complete reappraisal and readjustment. We have spoken of the pink-over-violet combination; we now refer to the violet-over-pink oil. Through personal experience, guided by intuition, backed up by many readings and consultations with those who have chosen this particular dual colour combination, I can say the following about it.

Within the pink of this combination there is a hint of magenta, faint but unmistakable. We are aware of pink as a begin-again colour, non-aggressive, representing unconditional love. Sometimes in the upreaching for the pure self, the pure mission, even the willingness to give unconditional love, there is a need for a healing within the person himself. The need may differ to some extent according to the person and circumstances, but it is invariably a need to love all that is going on around one rather than anything specific. Those striving for the ultimate (violet), seeking to pursue the depths, to find their own special mission and the freedom to do so, can sometimes be invaded by a feeling of frustration. This creates a loveless situation, however temporary, that seemingly envelops and saps the true emergence and freedom of the self. The pink searches for love, gives love, and yet, oh how much the magenta is needed – the upper region of the spectrum related to healing, incorporating the energies and demands of everyday life balanced with the heavenly upreaching of the soul and the mind. Bring the violet and magenta together, reinforce all that is surging and searching within one, feel the flow of unconditional love once more, healing and enhancing the very situation in which one struggles. Feel the glow and the stretch of the soul upwards and outwards, touch the fingertips that are always held out unseen, know yourself part of infinity and eternity. Place the precious oils upon you, anywhere at any time. This, child of love, is for yourself. For the love of others and their healing, place a little on the palms of your hands and give it to them. Where the light leads, healing on all levels must certainly follow.

Yin and yang come together in this oil, which is the loveliest and gentlest aspect of the blue-over-purple oil, the 'Rescue'. It will deal gently with physical emergency, and mental and spiritual turmoil, lightening the load.

Red-over-purple

One could say that this beautiful, rich combination brings heaven to earth. It shows an affinity of the soul life for earth existence. Clairvoyants, those with inner sight, resonate instinctively with it, for they use it as a r eans of transmission, in both receiving and giving.

The red-over-purple 'Balance' could also be regarded as a 'hot-line' to heaven. It is an oil connected with communication, the outreaching of the spirit. I look on it as a 'today' bottle, because it is associated with the here and now, and with the 'eternal now' which links the past, present and the immediate future. It will be mostly chosen at the end of the selection, and be either the third or the fourth choice (see page 91).

Clairvoyants and healers engaged in the range of healing in its broadest sense realize how much transmutation of energies is necessary for communication, direct or otherwise. One can see, therefore, the significance of the red in the top fraction, the life and earth energies. It is the life force, and, incidentally, provides the essential grounding that is a key factor when in touch with the higher consciousness. This red and violet combination is particularly valuable for ley-line cleansers, providing protection and direction. The oil should be especially applied to the feet and hands. In a room or building where poltergeist activity occurs or where there is an evil atmosphere, the vibrations of this oil can produce a strong protection. For those working with such problems, a protective application to the pulse areas of the wrists, and at night to the solar plexus is greatly recommended.

In respect of bodily health, this combination may be a great help in anaemia, and even in leukaemia, where there is a deficiency of haemoglobin in the blood. It may well be of use too in cases of mineral deficiency and imbalance of hormones.

This radiant red and violet oil when shaken changes to a beautiful rich plum colour, creating warmth and promise.

Pink-over-turquoise

Visually, this colour combination is very powerful. Where one's space is threatened, or in a relationship where love becomes possessive and the partner's space is confined, then this oil is a miracle worker for it helps create space and recycle the 'give and take' of love. It is inspirational for the creative. Children and young people would find this oil valuable as they often feel threatened by what they term 'the system', be it the authorities or the parents. They feel the threat of conditional love. We have all heard of, if not experienced, the 'unless you behave/conform, you will no longer receive love/privileges' ultimatum. True love knows no conditions of sale or bargaining.

The turquoise is closely connected to the blue-green of the emotional chakra, the heart, and literally should reach 'the heart of the matter'. It is therefore possible to see how emotional situations could be helped by the turquoise, itself a yin-and-yang colour containing both blue and green. Spiritually, it is a combination often chosen by people originally from other planets who have been born here in order to heal the earth. Physically, the pink-over-turquoise oil is for healing the heart and lungs and is especially helpful to asthmatics, freeing the lungs of all irritating invasion. It is excellent, too, for both the female and male reproductive areas and can be applied on all chakras where imbalance occurs.

Here I will pause a moment to address the sceptical. There is no science of the spirit, what I write about comes from 'inner tuition', and where this comes into play one ceases to try to rationalize that which is incapable of rational explanation. Bear with me then, accept what is acceptable to your inner being. I place a bowl of spiritual food before you. That which you cannot enjoy or digest put gently to one side; eat and digest that which you can. Perhaps at some future time, dear reader, you will have an appetite for the pieces you have put aside today. Simple folk, of no great education, who live close to the earth, guided by their instincts, with little to tease the fringes of the mind, have no difficulty in accepting the idea of an inner awareness.

Green-over-pink

The green-over-pink oil represents the gift of discernment, the forerunner of unconditional love, the giving and receiving of love. No aggressive thought can intrude here, no preconceived idea or prejudice, but simply the outpouring and inflow of love that remains constant for ever. Within this situation a soul may be at peace with a soul, in the complete absolution of love, and with the cleansing of both giver and receiver.

The green aspect puts all that is past and present in its true place, the pastures where sheep may safely graze. This love knows no bounds. The soul is free and the place is now ready for full occupation. It is the beginning of new life. Possessive love cannot enter here, for if this occurs the space is threatened and the recipient will have 'cramping' within his soul.

Green is the colour for the heart chakra and pink for unconditional love, so the combination truly manifests the deepest levels of love. Thus each of us is able really to care for himself and overcome his limitations, expressing, as we all wish to, God's love for mankind.

The green-over-pink bottle is valuable for epileptics, releasing the violence of the seizure through the pink and of the spasm through the green. It is also ideal, surely, for post-operative use – cancer operations, mastectomies, colostomies, or any other such operation where the person may feel invaded or degraded.

The value of pink is now well established for its ability to calm aggressiveness. It therefore helps in times of mental turmoil, resentments, inflammatory conditions and the feeling of being 'attacked'.

Yellow-over-pink

This is the 'begin again' oil, the 'rebirth' bottle, with the wisdom coming to channel the love within that is longing to get out. Time has taught many lessons but wisdom has not always been present. Let us step out of the shadow of the past and step boldly into the light of today, bringing new wisdom, new life, new promise – the fulfilment of the self, of the spirit, freedom of the mind to touch once more the areas in which guilts, mistakes and errors of judgement lie, all of which, at one time, have prevented complete fulfilment. Look once more upon yourself through this crystal reflection and see yourself as you came into life, with a purpose, to carry out in dedication. See yourself once more as you were before the world put its 'sticky fingers' upon you. Know forgiveness for yourself and for others.

On the physical level, the yellow-over-pink combination relates well to the endocrinal system and digestive tract. Hormonal imbalances, especially menopausal disharmonies or deficiencies, respond well to this oil. The pink's association with the uterus makes this doubly important to the female reproductive area.

Deep rose-over-deep pink

All the traumatic situations that can assail us in life – childlessness, divorce, bereavement, illness, the humiliation of unemployment – may lead to a build-up of hate, bitterness and resentment which never solve the problem but merely scar the soul. At such times, self respect and self belief disappear. A silent natural reaction, such as the secret feeling of guilt, however unmerited, creeps into the situation and the constant query of the battered mind is, 'Should I have?' or 'Could I have?'

Then rest upon the deep rose, child of love, feel the warmth once more of the divine unconditional love that will never leave you. Sink your whole being in the tenderness and gentleness of the pink below, seek for the real self, the reality of your destiny. Know within you that here is the crucifixion that precedes the resurrection, the beginning of the on-going life with its full purpose. The essential thing is to learn to love oneself again, dismissing all thoughts of guilt, lifting oneself above the situation, raising the body, mind and spirit. This is when the steel of the sword of the spirit is being tempered. Use it in conjunction with green that you may find your true place once more. Make the decisions that take you forward rather than taking the retrograde step of dwelling in the past. Look to the future and its promise of fulfilment.

As we have already found, pink is an anti-aggressive colour and therefore this particular combination has a two-way effect, stopping aggression both from within and without. It is easy to see, then, the value of this jewel to those with emotional troubles and to psychopaths. It is also a help to epileptics.

Ethereal pale pink-over-pale pink

This is the 'begin again, pick yourself up' oil, the one that could attract one's true soul mate, the whole beautiful concept of love. It is the promise of predestined, meet-again love. This lovely pale oil helps counteract the effects of 'un-love', placing one 'in the pink'. It is for one who needs love and has love to give. All gentle, sensitive souls will relate naturally to this oil.

Use this pale pink combination for hang-ups and irrational fears, the origins of which may reach back into childhood. Use it also against aggression, one's own or someone else's. The pale pink combination may be helpful for a person with a faded or weak aura, but ensure that a stronger colour such as the green is used in conjunction with the pink to give strength and backbone. This oil is valuable in anorexia, where one is subconsciously trying to alter one's image.

Purple-over-magenta

The purple-over-magenta oil denotes a person deeply aware of the spiritual, desiring to use the love within himself for healing through whatever medium. It is the lesson of love outpouring, of healing reaching out. It belongs to an 'old soul', definitely 'of the purple', the high sphere, the goddess, the priesthood, the dedicated, the St Teresas of life, the psychic, the inwardly perceptive. This is a person who has been to hell and back at times throughout the evolutionary period, who has been crucified, has learned to love himself and humanity again and seeks his mission to heal others through love and understanding. Because of this stretching of the soul, it could denote a well-balanced, courageous person who, through past suffering, has now developed a backbone where there might well have been a wishbone – not a wishful thinker but a seasoned sufferer.

The lovely purple/magenta oil is a purifier which brings understanding in its wake. It can assist the development of intuition and spiritual faculties. On the physical and mental levels it aids recovery from and renewal after illness and/or operations – the magenta to restore energy and the purple to help restore the potassium/sodium balance. This delightful oil soothes frayed nerves, can help the disillusioned to see things in true perspective and, indeed, can benefit the entire endocrine system.

Red-over-green and green-over-red

> *Perfect love casteth out fear.*
> 1 John 4:18

Two of the most interesting, revealing and diagnostic colour combinations are direct opposites of one another – the red-over-green oil (masculine) and the green-over-red oil (feminine), which for easy identification have been termed 'Robin Hood' and 'Maid Marion'. These oils consist of two contrasting colours, each providing for the need of the other, each supplying the demand of the masculine or the feminine aspect of our nature.

Pure harmony and full function of all faculties on all levels can be obtained only when the being is able to transmute the natural desires and earth energies. Masculine aggressiveness must be modulated and transformed through the nurturing of such feminine qualities as intuition and gentleness. In the male, it is the red quality that creates the transmutation of true self. The red-over-green combination is the mirror of the physical male with the pressures upon him to produce and take the leadership role in this life. These cause any latent femininity to be involuntarily suppressed, fearing an impediment to self-expression. Society has created a strict line of demarcation between what are regarded as male and female qualities. The whole concept of the dominant male and his related duties has been programmed into his very thinking. He has been conditioned from the cradle. But true creativity is represented by the *womb*, and the perfect balance of the being is in the recognition and harmonizing within oneself of both the male and female aspects. Thus can complete fulfilment of being be obtained – there need be no loss of status or power.

The green base fraction is the mirror and expression of the space which needs to be given to the feminine in the male, the woman – 'womb-man' – within. Only in the renunciation of the all-male comes the realization of the whole 'wo-man' man.

'Maid Marion', the green-over-red 'Balance', and normally an oil chosen by a female, indicates again the position within which the being has entered incarnation. Just as the male is mirrored in the red-over-green combination, so the female is mirrored by the green-over-red oil. Gentle, caring qualities have been nurtured within the woman by society. The duties expected of her reflect, naturally, the fact that she has been designed by nature to become mother as well as lover.

Mankind, in common with the birds and mammals, has nesting periods with all their duties and devotions. We hear in the Song of Solomon (2.10 and 12) that beautiful love call: 'Rise up, my love, my fair one, and come away ... the time of the singing of birds is come.'

This is a lovely moment, a function, a fulfilment. Nevertheless, the moment passes, the nest empties and the fledglings, now fully grown, seek their own fulfilment. The love grouping is still there, the silver cord of love is firmly fixed, but the time of the singing of birds is come for the offspring. Primarily, the woman is forever creative and the soul does not become extinct at the flight of the young. How many mothers at this time experience a feeling of devastation with the sudden notion that fulfilment is no longer on-going. Have no fear, it is only the soul stretching. After the body, the spirit seeks its own fulfilment. Well known and medically acknowledged is the menopausal depressive state and its accompanying ailments. Pills and potions solve no problem, for here the root cause is the stultification of the soul.

The panacea 'find yourself another interest' serves to pass time. But timelessness is calling.

In a relationship between a man and a woman based on unconditional love, absolute faith and loyalty exists. As with the give-and-take in physical love, so it should be in spiritual love. One should not feed the body and starve the soul. There is no need for the man of middle years to seek reassurance of his virility with other partners, likewise the female need not create liaisons to re-establish her self-esteem.

In any situation where she is dominated, the female should be encouraged to use the reverse combination, the red-over-green oil. The male, if dominated, would probably betray this diagnostically in his choice of the green-over-red. Here it is a case of again introducing the fight-back element. I have noticed with interest how many times during the free choice of selection of 'Balance' bottles one can detect the sensitive male (green-over-red oil). He is the one likely to be dominated, but who is creative and spiritually sensitive. Then there is the female, over-feminized, gentle, loving, a 'door-mat', who is prone to being dominated. For her the red is so important.

The green in both combinations has its particular purpose. Green is of course the space-giver, the decision-maker, the 'I know where I'm going' colour, the 'go hug a tree' that is essential in many situations, the space where a soul may stretch. A cross-roads? Then cross it. Green by itself or in any form or combination is important, helping to avoid the 'I wish' thoughts.

Red-over-blue and blue-over-red

As in the previous two combinations, both these oils are complementary, bringing together heaven and earth.

Those who travel in the astral plane or do work connected with the etheric realm find these two oils an efficacious accompaniment. In healing, yoga, meditation, levitation of the spirit and in aspiration, their value is unlimited. Where the physical body is concerned, the red-over-blue oil is the replacement unit, the giver when anything is lacking. When shaken, it comes together as a beautiful violet and thus is appropriate as a healer in many respects. It gives a good protection for the spiritually-based who may be vulnerable to energy sapping by those around them.

One phrase falls into place with the blue-over-red oil: 'Peace on earth and good will to all men' – a worthy note in all peace projects. This is a beautiful balancing oil, especially valuable for re-earthing. The red will earth the mental airiness of the blue, and thus clairvoyants and yoga students will find it is of tremendous worth. It should also be used after meditation.

In describing the various 'Balance' combinations, I have sought only to open the mind of the reader to reveal the casket of brilliant jewels that lies within. Each one of us has the necessary inner perception; it is the gift to all whose fingertips and hearts stretch gently but hungrily towards the deeper, intimate knowledge of self-revelation. Wander within the jewels before you. They have a language; learn it. They are a book within themselves; read it and know that in the end they are the mirror held before you, and yours is the miracle.

The Signs and Symbols in Aura-Soma 'Balance'

There is in me a hesitancy born of awe and respect for the unknown, and so I find it particularly hard to expound upon the signs and symbols displayed in the 'Balance' bottles when they are shaken. The little miracles that occur apparently unbidden before one's eyes write with unseen hands a story within the jewels. I must therefore ask for your tolerance and understanding as I attempt to put into words that which is almost beyond words.

Symbolism has always existed and been used in all religions and cults throughout the ages. Even early Stone Age people expressed their deepest thoughts through drawings and signs in caves. Esoteric though it seems, symbolism conveys through a special power of its own the message that is needed.

The upper fraction denotes the thoughts and feelings in the present consciousness, of the purpose that lies within the base. It represents the conscious mind while the base denotes the 'unconscious' or subconscious underlying tendencies.

The left side of the upper fraction relates to the feminine aspect of self, the intuitive compassionate side. The right side of the upper fraction relates to the masculine analytical wisdom aspects. The mid-line between the upper and lower parts represents the essence or life line running through that which we know consciously and that which we only suspect.

After shaking the bottle, coalescing bubbles are occasionally seen to form one or more pyramidal shapes. When these appear in the left upper fraction they seem to indicate a connection with ancient Egypt, knowledge and experience from those days having been assimilated into the mind of the person.

In dreams and meditation there are no boundaries. The

magic carpet is within oneself. Time disappears, distance has no meaning or measure, the soul is free. There are times when we inwardly seek to re-visit places and spaces that have a bearing on our present lives. The soul, which travels with its vast accumulation of karma and wisdom gathered as it evolved, hungers for its own past experiences and seeks to glean these when the need is greatest.

Dreams are vehicles carrying memories, spiritual, physical and emotional, since the beginning of time, and sometimes give a glimpse into the future. At this stage I feel I must warn that care should be taken not to get 'hung up' on these forms and shapes within the beautiful jewels of 'Balance'. If we do, we might well end up like the two psychiatrists who, dealing perpetually with others' problems, greet each other in the street, 'How are you?' followed immediately before the answering response by, 'How am I?' Introspection, if it borders on the neurotic, could act as a barrier against facing the actuality of life. Wisdom and knowledge help only when used correctly. Like so many things, 'Balance' can be misused.

The right side in the upper level corresponds to mental activities associated with the right side of the brain. A pyramid appearing here denotes the search for wisdom because of the affinity with the pyramid period. Sometimes seen clearly detached above the pyramid is what could appear to be the golden dome of Mecca, which can be taken as an entitlement to embark on a spiritual visit to the ancient wisdom which once was available to that person.

On the physical level, the crystal bottle can be regarded as the outline of the skeletal body. The mid-line depicts the waist-line, the top oil represents the upper level of the body with its respective organs and disorders, and the region below the mid-line denotes the body from the solar plexus down. Although we speak of the physical, we must always bear in mind that the physical is linked with the spiritual and emotional nature and that no separate part of the human being is an island unto itself.

Physically, a pyramid on the mid-line, resting on the solar plexus, might well indicate a need for physical adjustment either in a block stemming from the digestive region, or nutritionally. Here it might be advisable to adjust the diet. Needless to say, this is but the tip of the iceberg and the rest is yours to explore, to touch and to know.

Striations – straight lines usually on the top level of the bottle – are there as if to show an upstretching to bring into this life that which touches a higher level, the silent longings for the Higher Consciousness. Very often around these striations, or sometimes on its own, a cobwebby substance appears, representative of, I feel, all the karmas, cloudings, unhappiness, and turbulence of the past being cleared as the upreaching continues. Ultimately it can only be for the good, for when that which was can come through the mists of time to reach into the present life, the top level of the bottle, it can only indicate karmic clearance, a time to sing.

Many are the different kinds of formation, each with an interpretation. I give you but a guideline to some of them. The rest I leave to the greater guide within you, and the Godhead.

Various large bubbles will tend to appear. If a solitary bubble occurs on either side of the bottle just above the mid-line, it could indicate opposing forces, separations, or a mind unable to decide. Do not confuse this with the energy levels and turmoils which were mentioned in the previous chapter.

A fuzzy cloud running the whole length of the mid-line indicates a crossroads, a 'make your mind up' time, one which must be met and decided upon. I suggest that at such an indication, the all-green 'Balance' oil should be applied, or the gold-over-green combination used liberally so that the decision may be made wisely.

A cloudiness in the top fraction is often observed in those who have a problem, spiritual, mental or physical. On the spiritual level, one's perceptions are being clouded by the mind which is seeking to rationalize what can never be rationalized. On the mental and physical levels, it is often an indication of inner trauma, disturbance, or mental confusion, but it could also be attributed to traumas and break-downs due to outer circumstances, situations that have suddenly become unbalanced or depressing.

A concave bow in the top half of the bottle could be an indication of imbalance in the thoracic cavity, and the chakra could well be reinforced and rebalanced by use of the blue/green 'Balance' oil.

At the neck of the bottle, representing the communication chakra, which is connected with the throat, mouth, and head, bubbles or a line right at that top level can be dealt with best through the all-blue 'peace' 'Balance' or the 'Rescue', the blue-over-purple oil, for here there is a need to free the communication centre to allow free flow from the fontenelles through the 'third eye'. Clearance of bubbles at this level could help create freedom, clarity of speech and thought in the future.

The lower fraction, from the spiritual aspect, represents the soul in its spiral 'evolvement' through time. The very first indication of time regression in a person can be the appearance of a graph-like structure adhering to and pointing down from the mid-line. Large formations of bubbles, usually rimmed, reaching downwards in varying degrees, depict the turmoils and karmic situations throughout the 'evolvement'. Please do remember that the value of the interpretations and represen-tations should not be used for entertainment, but should be used rather as a cleansing agent for areas of karmic distur-bance, the pus pockets that fester within that need to be known, shown and disposed of. With the emptying of these pockets comes self-recognition, new thought, new life, new power, and the soul can travel once more in safety and freedom. In the hands of a good regressive therapist this can be achieved.

Flashbacks in time, recurrent patterns that are experienced as nightmares, can be seen as cobwebs hanging in the upper and lower fractions. The dredging up, termed 'bleeding', of the base colour into the top fraction has often been interpreted as the past influencing the present, as things not resolved in the past that are being brought up in the present.

As I write, I am shown a particularly interesting phenomenon. A therapist presents a blue-over-purple 'Balance' that shows upon shaking something that has not been mentioned before. There is a throwing up of the purple which lies on the mid-line into the blue top fraction. It stays there for quite a time, as if struggling to break through the barrier and the block, then it falls back into the past, the base of the bottle. I see this as the struggling of the past, the healing capability endeavouring to break through the barriers and shortfalls of this life with its disappointments. The young healer waits for the miracle that, if he did but know it, waits for him! There is a block to be removed, then full power will be released.

Mentally, the same striations or bubbles that lie between the mid-line and the bottom show the influence of the past in a present situation or that knowledge is sought from the past that it may be used wisely in the future. Pentagons appear, indicating the traveller in time, the space dweller, the wanderer, the healer, the wise men of the East, as it were, seeking the star.

Physically, as in the top level, so it is below, but in reverse. Instead of the concave shape that appears in the top fraction, we are now looking at the convex formation of bows in the bottom level. The depth to which the bow reaches corresponds with the physical location of organs in the body. Thus if the bow should literally reach the base of the bottle, it indicates the base of the spine, the coccyx or legs. Sometimes that in itself shows a need for complete chakra balancing, for the spine is the control centre of the whole length of the back and free movement and free flowing is essential on all chakra levels. It has been suggested that the Aura-Soma 'Rescue' and the green oils used concurrently seem to fit the need here.

The next bow up deals with the reproductive organs, the womb, gonads, the drive. Then we reach the liver, kidney and bladder and move higher to the navel. A bow just slightly higher would indicate that a balancing was needed in the digestive tract and solar plexus.

Pregnancy can be shown by an oval shape crossing the mid-line in the centre of the bottle, sometimes enclosing a lovely 'tadpole' or foetus shape in its centre. If the head of the foetus shape points below the mid-line with the tail reaching up comet fashion, it shows the coming in of an old soul, a special soul, a New Age child destined and programmed for the healing of this time but who has also known life elsewhere in the universe.

Clouding in the lower fraction is the indication of karmic violence or aggression against the soul in the past, or of one who has experienced aggression in the past of this life. The 'Pomander' is invaluable here (see page 159), and pink should be applied and worn for a period until a feeling of security, freedom and well-being returns.

The New Age Child

There is in each of us an innate knowledge of a Higher Consciousness controlling and directing the life force. Man from the beginning of time has worshipped according to his degree of spiritual evolution. Common in primitive societies was ancestor worship, which was the religion in ancient China, for example. The earliest representations of ancient Egyptian deities in the form of animal or bird appeared long before the first hieroglyphs, and these gradually gave way to gods in human form. Animism, the belief that inanimate objects (rivers, trees, etc.) and natural phenomena (sun, wind, rain) have living souls, was common in many societies. Ra – the sun – sovereign of the sky, was just one of the many deities to whom the Egyptians paid homage. The Incas of Peru worshipped a creator-god and after him the sun, moon, thunder and a multitude of rocks and trees. The sun was the personal god of the Inca, occupying a major place in the state religion and playing an important part in the consolidation of their empire. Little is known of the Druid religion, but from the writings of Pliny and Julius Caesar we learn that Druids worshipped in oak groves and probably paid homage to the powers of nature.

Many early civilizations functioned in such a way that the king, the head of society, was also an incarnation of the god. Was it, in fact, the deep inner knowledge and recognition of the Godhead within oneself? Man has a need to worship, but the religious terms he chooses are only important to him in so far as he can relate to them. Thus there are many names of gods, many religions and many sects but all lead to the One Light.

The Essences are each a separate glass
Through which Being's Light is passed –
Each tinted fragment sparkles in the sun
A thousand colours –
But the Light is One.

Lao Tse

The child of today, born at the threshold of the long-awaited Age of Aquarius, is a very special child, being the herald of the New Age. A great many souls incarnating today are programmed for a purpose and have been called from the four corners of the earth, and indeed from the entire universe – old souls, teachers, masters, healers from space, leaders all.

Recently I heard an interesting statement on a tape recording by Dr Guy Manners, about the measuring of vibrations. He said that the vibrations of people today are rising rapidly. The significance of this, I feel, has a bearing on the New Age, particularly in relation to the child born within the last few years. This child comes in with experience gathered from many lifetimes, is acclimatized to higher vibrations, and is well able to carry out his mission within the higher levels.

Such a child comes in with perfect balance, which means first of all that he lives the normal life of a child, and so is well earthed. God does not rob His chosen ones of their childhood, their chance to grow and experience. How shall they relate if they do not experience? This is their 'growing up and growing into' time. Their hidden knowledge and memory banks await the ultimate release. Observe them for, although they appear as normal children, there is a quality about them that is quite different. These are the children that my father spoke of, protected against 'becoming so heavenly that they end up no earthly use'.

It is my belief that those adults who appear 'off-balance', who seem inexplicably vicious and corrupt, are the product of their inability to cope with the higher vibrations thrust upon them without due preparation. On a purely physical level, it has been found that certain refined foods and food additives can cause a hyperactive or aggressive response in some individuals, especially children. It occurs to me, then, that if food for the physical being can create such dreadful disharmony, how much more havoc can be wrought through unaccustomed spiritual vibration, the food of the soul?

One night in meditation I received my instructions. An additional 'Balance' was about to be born, a complete chakra colour set specifically for the New Age child, the promise for the future. The heavenly silver cord was to be represented by the top fraction, clear, unencumbered by any earthly intrusion, relating to the spiritual, an indication of the higher vibrations now coming in. The lower base fraction represented as usual a chakra colour. It is a progressive 'Balance' designed to guide, develop and protect the child, from the moment of conception right along his or her path of evolvement. There are seven such vessels of precious oils, each one symbolizing the progress of the child within the seven pillars of wisdom, answering the particular needs of each growing period.

For guidance as to which 'Balance' combinations to use, and when, I have set these out for the seven periods of life as I feel and see them. However, there is a greater guide within you. Sometimes an inner instinct will tell you when another oil would be more beneficial. Obey this, for in the obedience lies the seal of faith.

The gold-over-red 'Balance', the sunset bottle, is the oil to use for the conception of the special child. For those who want to conceive and bring in a special soul, the act of coitus must be lifted above the mere physical act. Desire must become perfectly balanced with wisdom and tenderness, and a complete spiritual unity be created within the loving couple. In that harmony the waiting soul may enter with joy and without fear. Their harmonious loving thoughts actually create an energy that surrounds the conception. That energy has a colour, which attracts the soul of the child to the fertilized egg.

The blue-over-pink 'Balance' oil, the 'peace and love' bottle, is a very special combination and of great importance to true balance. This lovely combination represents the realization of the two 'fractions' within us all, the masculine and feminine, the quiescent, responsive, nurturing qualities of yin perfectly balanced by the fiery dynamism of yang.

So God created man in his own image, in the image of God created he him; male and female created he them.

Gen. 1:27

The allegorical reference to the rib of Adam being used to create Eve surely was an indication that the two aspects of being were from within one body.

The blue-over-pink oil is an aid to balanced development of both aspects of being, neither denying the one nor retarding the other. It is a realization oil. Many resonate to it as an aura colour and, when chosen as such, it is an indication of a perfectly balanced person. It is creative. As the child comes from the mother's womb (the cradle of creation represented by the pink fraction), so the need for channelling is centralized and given direction by the masculinity of the blue, thus establishing a purpose for the creativity.

This lovely oil is known as the New Age child's 'Rescue' bottle. In fact, it is a more subtle version of the blue-over-purple oil, the Aura-Soma adult 'Rescue'. As such, the blue/pink oil can be used on babies or mothers during pregnancy; it is excellent for both. Let the child or young person who needs harmony and completeness use this combination, for it is an essential aid to 'finding oneself'. To the young girl who needs to be more assertive, or the small boy who needs to be more caring, it brings love and peace. Use it as a protection against emotional crisis and as a preparation before entering stressful situations. An application once a week will serve both as a protector and a cleanser.

Now we move on to the New Age child set of 'Balance' bottles, five beautiful combinations each with a clear silver upper fraction. The silver (clear) in any of the combinations is the symbol of clarity, the silver cord, the ever-present link with the Divine within us all, giving clearness of vision and purpose, and spiritual awareness. It is unmarred by materiality, and is directed through the silver cord relating intimately with the crown of the head wherein is held the ancient memories and wisdom. Clouding in this fraction will occur when situations are not in complete harmony. When that occurs, the consolation,

I believe, is literally a cleansing of the situation through the vibrations held within the oils. The silver portrays the beginning of the soul's spiral journey, untrammelled and untouched as yet by karma. In its absolute purity and purpose, it represents the unsullied soul before life's journey places its sticky fingers upon it.

Silver-over-pink

First let us consider the silver/pink combination, an oil of deep spiritual love. During the infant's first tender months, when the fontanelles are not yet closed, the child is still attuned to the infinite and should be kept thus while information is being fed into the memory bank of this precious vessel. God says to His angels: 'We will not close this cavity in the skull until we have fed in for one whole year all the memories of the past and knowledge for the future, that it may be released when they come to their time of wisdom.' The physical body of the child develops along its own lines, preparing the framework that is to support the true being for the rest of this incarnation.

Little girls will relate to this exquisite, clear pink oil. The old saying 'pink for a girl and blue for a boy' has its foundation in actual truth. (I understand, though, that in Belgium the saying is reversed!) Femininity has always been expressed through the soft, gentle, loving colour of pink, signifying too the protectiveness of the mother who instinctively nurtures and guards the child against aggression.

The silver/pink 'Balance' is the 'love thyself' oil. During the soul's progression, hard experiences and the formation of karma leads to much self love being lost. The tender soul finds itself sometimes pushed through circumstances or desires into the wrong channel of spiritual development, sailing as it were under false colours. It is during this traumatic time, when love and respect for self is lost, when inwardly one knows that the true being has been betrayed, that psychological 'projections' begin. If you are not in love with yourself, how shall you love others, your neighbours? Will you not surely project upon them all the frustrations, failures and regrets that colour your life, and the hate of the betrayal of your inner being? Will you not silently accuse them of all you hate most in yourself, for have they not become a mirror of yourself? To love oneself is to unlock the door to loving others and being loved in return. The silver/pink 'Balance', the 'love thyself' bottle – you, as you were, as you can be and as you shall be – is the remedial oil that should be used regularly to grant self-esteem, knowledge of the true self and clarity of vision. So many people have remarked on the change in themselves and their situation after using this gentle oil.

A person in adult life, reaching for a clear vision of love, both in giving and receiving, would use this oil. And it may benefit not only those with difficulties resulting from unsolved childhood problems but also those with any illness that falls into the general category of psychosomatic.

Silver-over-blue

> *Let me take your hand*
> *That I may share with you*
> *The peace of heavenly blue,*
> *That love's dear hand*
> *May welcome you and*
> *Place a royal crown*
> *Upon your head.*

Edna Holford

The silver-over-blue 'Balance' oil relates to the boy child, helping him to establish his identity. This is a gentle blue, bringing in the quieter element that is needed sometimes with the more rumbustious boy. With an over-active, even aggressive child, the feminine aspect of pink should be applied on occasion to re-establish the balance that has been disturbed. Conversely, the silver/blue oil can be used for the girl child who lacks assertiveness or confidence, or is even perhaps a lazy feeder as a baby, thus granting the greater measure of assertiveness that is obviously necessary. Should this same lack of confidence arise with a boy, then a darker blue, perhaps with a hint of red, might be indicated. The Aura-Soma adult 'Rescue', the blue-over-purple oil, would fit the bill admirably.

On the physical level, the silver/blue or the full 'peace' bottle, the all-blue oil, can be used during fevers, fretful periods and during any of the infectious illnesses that children go through. We have found that even visually it seems to bring peace, calm and cooling to its surroundings, so it may prove a boon in the sickroom.

In adolescence, it can impart a deeper sense of purpose and inner tranquillity, and is good for anyone seeking peace and clarity. It may help the adult who needs to examine his child-hood in order to become fully awakened to the present. It can also be a sign that one is clearing the clutter from one's life in pursuance of a deeper spiritual purpose. Often those engaged in any form of healing, including the healing of themselves, find help from this particular combination.

Silver-over-green

> Let me take your hand
> For gentle touch
> Will make a space
> For minds to meet
> In love's sweet hold,
> And you may rest
> Upon the tender green.

Edna Holford

Next we deal with the silver-over-green 'Balance' combina-tion. There is a stage that most mothers are aware of, when the child is literally trying to find its own space by touching, reach-ing, investigating everything and everywhere. It is sometimes referred to as the age of the 'terrible twos'. Parents and grand-parents feel that a small demolition squad has arrived in their midst, and all precious objects are moved up out of range of tiny fingers.

Whereas the silver fraction enables the child to find his or her spiritual position (for in these formative years he must be held closely to the spiritual place from whence he came), the green helps the child to know himself, his place in this world and gives inner knowledge of his relationship to the spiritual.

Green is a colour that aids decision-making and clarity of thought. It relates very well to the 'make your mind up' time or when one reaches a cross-roads in life. There is a stage in all our lives when we must know where we are going and with whom, forgetting the whys and wherefores and going forward firmly, in faith. Green is the chakra colour known as the space-giver, or place-giver, and in this context it helps give the confidence to relax our concepts, attitudes and postures so that, together with the silver, an expanding consciousness leading to greater harmony with our surroundings can be experienced. It has been said that, on a lower level of thought, green can induce material gains. However, on a higher level, I feel that if the space is right, the place is right and the right decision has been made then everything will flow naturally.

Woodland sprites, born of the woods with an affinity to Mother Earth and her creatures, dedicated animal lovers and, incidentally, animal healers, all have a deep need for green. There is life within life in the woods, and the mysteries there are revealed only to those with eyes to see and ears to hear. Clairvoyants relate to green, for their sight is not as others.

This oil eases claustrophobia and is often chosen by people who feel restricted by routine work or enclosed spaces – the self-encapsulated and the nine-to-five workers. The indecisive can receive so much from any green combination, and the silver/green oil can be substituted for any of the other heart chakra oils or used in conjunction with them.

Silver-over-gold

> Let me take your hand
> That we may find the way
> With love's pure gold
> To ease your pain,
> Uplift your heart,
> Unlock your soul
> To wisdom's ray.

> Edna Holford

This period in a child's life, with its broadening horizons and wider outreaching in relationships involving schoolfriends, teachers and ultimately girl and boyfriends, calls for greater wisdom and protection. Parents are well aware of sometimes having to stand back slightly during this period as they see their children stepping forward into life. They, mindful of the pitfalls, temptations, hurts and disillusionments that lie before their offspring, find that, in the desire to share, protect and guide, the weapon of words is useless. Further aggravating the situation is the growing child's desire to make it alone, as an individual in his own right, needing yet pushing away the very help that comes from the heart. This is their time, their growing period. Often I have felt that there is a mutual need for wisdom here, for the child and the parents, and that the application of gold for wisdom applies to all and should be used by all, linking child with parents and with the silver cord, to protect and guide them all.

We have now reached the time, in adolescence or young adulthood, when what was given at this earth birth, before the fontanelles closed, can be channelled wisely. The memory bank of the past is the link to the future. Now the youngster can draw upon the silver cord gift of his or her memory bank and use it in the present, and use it well.

Remember, the gold in any combination in the top fraction relates to and supplies wisdom. Gold-over-green gives the wisdom to choose and use one's space and place correctly. Gold-over-red gives a balancing wisdom for the channelling of earth and the sexual energies. Gold-over-blue gives wisdom for the healer, bringing peace and harmony to the whole being.

Silver-over-violet

And now we come to the silver-over-violet oil. We have reached the time when the child with all his ingathering of earthly experiences, his temptations, glorious moments and dismal failures, needs not only to 'get it together' to lift himself to his rightful level, using all that has gone before, but also to endeavour not to lose it, and instead to use it. If one tries to bury these experiences, be sure that they will be dredged up as dark moments at unwanted times, resulting in hang-ups, pegs on which to hang excuses and resentments. Experiences, good or bad, are growing experiences and should be put to use.

The violet is upreaching but giving perfect balance between heaven and earth, leading to clear thought and objectivity about the individual's true role and mission in life. For the teenage child, it is a protection perhaps, a balancing that is needed to prevent the earthly pulls now awakening from completely swamping the harmony of the true being. Violet, an uplifting, protective colour, gives resistance to the lower temptation levels and yet allows full awareness of the need for earth energies in their entirety, helping to give a little heaven to balance the soul on earth.

For the adult, when we look at this oil do we not see the visionary, the creative artist, the poet, the scribe with his pen mightier than the sword? Do we not also see the healer? When I say 'healer', I stress that I use this word from the point of view of all aspects of healing, from all its sources in all worlds, seen and unseen. Our seeking soul – for as it was said, a man's reach should always exceed his grasp – is ever reaching upwards within us, however much we try to silence it. Meditation and the opening of the 'third eye' are much influenced through this colour. It is important to remember to place red somewhere in the vicinity too, for 'earthing'. So when meditating with the pure violet oil, it is essential to have the full red 'Balance' or a red combination oil within the room or upon the feet or hands for 'earthing' purposes. However high one travels in time and spirit, one's feet must remain on the ground.

The silver/violet oil is the spiritual version of the Aura-Soma 'Rescue', the blue-over-purple combination, bringing clarity within meditation, purity in thought and the wisdom of old souls. It promotes calmness, clarity and good judgement on all levels, the material, emotional and the spiritual. It is an invaluable antidote to aggressiveness and bitterness and helps in the treatment of the mentally disturbed, getting them together on all levels – for here, although the soul has knowledge of its own harmony, the mind and the body have become disjointed. The silver/violet combination is a protection against the need for artificial stimulants such as drugs, alcohol and all excesses and abuses. They may stimulate the body but they destroy the soul.

This set of spiritual 'Balance' oils has been brought into being not only for the 'Balance' child but for the 'off-balance' person, as through them the root cause can be reached and treated, and the true self be revealed. Alcoholics, drug addicts, the violent, possessed, depressed, frustrated and desperate, all those who are not relating to their true selves, and to the Godhead within each one of them, are all likely to receive help through these combinations.

Essences, Pomanders and Quintessences

A dark flame arose in the most secret recess from the mystery of Ain Soph, the Infinite, like a vapour that takes shape from the shapeless, encircled by the sphere's ring, neither white nor black, red nor green, nor of any colour. As the flame began to take form it produced radiant colours. A source welled up out of it and spread over everything below.

From The Zohar

The knowledge I had learned at the apothecary shop was not to be abandoned and lost when I became a chiropodist. I continued to gather herbs and flowers, extracting their essences for use in my healing creams and lotions and eventually in 'Balance' oils. At Kings Ransom we grew aromatic plants for this purpose. I used only live plants, never anything dried.

From my father I had learned that these living energies should be taken only when the time was right. Those that were ready, full of their virtue, I took when the sun shone in a final farewell or when the dew had fallen like a benediction upon them.

Having plucked them with prayer they would then be placed, like a child, within the womb of the mother and became a suspension of unconditional love. In this suspension, like a child waiting to emerge, they would await their time. Reaching their full term, they would then come forth and enter into their new life, their reincarnation.

While at Kings Ransom, under inspiration, I made special collections of plant essences in demijohns, an inheritance from the pharmacy. Each demijohn contained 49 extracts and essences, though the proportion within each one varied. After we left Kings Ransom I took my 'babies', as I called them, with me and continued to add to them. They waited their purpose, their time to come. Some 15 years later, after 'Balance' was born, I suddenly received the instruction, 'Send out these living energies, these plants, it is their time now to come forth.'

That is how the Aura-Soma Pocket Pomander came into being. There are several varieties now, as well as the original, each with a different colour, their true purpose yet to be revealed.

The name Pomander was given during the Dark Ages, formalising a method of emitting vapours for protective and healing purposes. Since the beginning of man's awareness incense has been used by the priesthood of religious cults. Sacred herbs in the midst of a pierced nut were used by the Incas. In Elizabethan times a bouquet of herbs was given to judges in the common court to overcome pollutive and infectious invasion. Herbal pomanders were used as a protection during the Plague but many of the mysterious sacred substances were lost in time with their meanings obscured. The vapours became a far cry from the circle of Creation. Aura-soma has rediscovered the original vapours in her Pomanders with the numerological significance of 49 – seven times seven symbolic herbs within each and every sacred vapour released.

Poisonous substances are being poured onto the earth and plants today seem to know that they are under threat. Essences prepared recently when compared to those existing 20 years ago seem more aggressive and slightly acrid. People too seem more aggressive, perhaps intuitively conscious of a menace in the atmosphere.

The Aura-Soma Pomander came into being just before our second visit to Denmark in April 1986. It was at the time of the Chernobyl disaster and Scandinavia lay in the path of the fall-out. So severe was the fall-out that before we had realized it had happened Mike and I commented on the soreness of our lips and throats. Applying the 'Pocket Rescue' intuitively, we found that the symptoms were alleviated. Upon hearing what had happened we then used the Pomander to help clear the pollution. The Pomander and the Pocket Rescue came into their own.

At the end of an exhibition where we had a stand, the atmosphere was heavy. Among the visitors were drug-takers and smokers and the organizers had some people walking around with bunches of herbs to dispel the heaviness, no doubt on the principle of the Judge's Bouquet. Perhaps the combination of herbs was not correct for it was not working. I sent Mike Booth with one or two helpers around with Pomanders. The organizers came up to our stand and commented on the improvement in the atmosphere, incidentally purchasing a few Pomanders. Since then we have always made a point of using them when the atmosphere is threatening.

To use the Pomander, apply to the palms of the hands and then pass over the head and around the periphery of the body thus granting protection to the chakras and the electromagnetic field. Many are now using this method of protection and the demand from home and abroad is increasing daily.

Another powerful vapour released for the New Age is the 'Master Quintessence'. Each Quintessence comes in a beautiful pale tone and contains special essences. It works on a higher level than the Pomander and is applied on the wrist pulses and then passed around the head and over the frontal and auric aspect of the body thus opening the intuitive and spiritual perceptions within the being. It has been referred to as 'the hot line to heaven', forming a bridge between the user and the spiritual Master to whom he or she relates, the one who has the same wavelength and is attuned to the user's soul group.

Although 'Balance' differs from the Pomander and Quintessence in that it is applied to the skin while the Pomanders and Quintessences emit fragrant vapours, in all three, colour is the key that opens the door to the wavelengths of the body.

To return to the plant kingdom, certain plants have spiritual access to the 'Greater Garden of Being' and can go backwards and forwards over the bridge. The beautiful rose, especially, goes back and forth in her season. They all know her in the Garden. The love she personifies is the unconditional love she encounters on the other side and brings back with her to earth.

Throughout the years since childhood the colours of flowers

– the outward portrayal of their inner virtue, the essence of their being, their aura, their soul – have always held a special fascination for me. I believe, and I have heard this belief echoed, that flowers and animals (including humans) have a language of their own and a means of communication.

If one accepts 'scientific' evidence, plants respond to colours and music, and also to conversation between them and human beings. Music, it appears, gives rise to movement within the plants. Flowers flourish on love and conversation and recycle it through their own beauty, thereby showing their love. Do not the flowers themselves reach up with all their essence to find the light, as we do? Is there not an answering call to the very centre of their being, as there is with us? Do they not give their lives gladly, for are they not presented at the three most important happenings in the human life cycle – birth, death and marriage, and as an expression of love? Giving is theirs as surely as it is ours. They struggle, as we do, that colour may be brought back into the world, that healing and love may reign. The soul of the flower is supreme in its giving and spiritual in what it seeks to obtain.

It was gradually born in upon me, when among my beloved flowers and herbs, that I was beginning the process of giving them eternal life, even as my father had before me. Through the giving of themselves for the healing and happiness of others, they make a true sacrifice of love. It is their entitlement, as it is ours, to fulfil their beauty on earth and to live eternally thereafter. Would it be beyond the bounds of possibility that the flower which sacrificed itself on the altar of love might one day become part of the very soul for which it had been sacrificed? Could we not further suppose that in the final supreme giving of its life, the flower becomes part of the Godhead?

When preparing flower essences I would sometimes find the colour of the flower reflected in the colour of the essence and sometimes it would remain colourless. When this is the case one finds an affinity within the colour related flowers, fruit or leaves indicating the chakra or station with which it is involved. For example: lavender – head chakra; golden calendula – epidermis, nervous system, stomach; etc. I began to realize that the colour associated with the plant had an affinity with the human chakra colours.

Red

Red is the stimulator, the energizer, and is connected with passion, ambition, the basic emotions, sex drive, and all that is 'earthy', without which life would have no continuity, the leader no drive nor the healer any grounding. Astrologically, Mars relates to red; the Leo person needs red for uplift and will very often select red, combined perhaps with gold, as a 'Balance' choice. A clairvoyant leans upon red to provide energies for the unseen guides to draw upon when seeking communication.

Of the colour-related essences, clearly that of the red rose is the accepted symbol of love. Hypericum, or St John's Wort, which has reddish stems and berries, produces a most beautiful red when oil is added. Rose geranium is wonderful, for it brings grounding into the spiritual part of love, thus bringing about complete balance. Ylang-ylang, much loved by the Chinese, is so re-energizing that it has been referred to as nature's aphrodisiac. Here, too, we must mention the beloved bergamot, which fosters harmony when used in conjunction with most of her related essences.

On the physical level, these red-related essences bring healing, setting in motion energies already within one. They bring much needed earth energies, and they bring love. These particular essences are embodied within the all-red 'Balance' oil, and indeed, within all the red-based combinations in the Aura-Soma 'Balance' range.

Pink

The pink-related essence is closely connected with female qualities, the uterus, and the creative and unconditional love so well known to woman ('womb-man'). It is clearly expressed within the essence of the rose – that beautiful shell pink – and the rose geranium. The pink of mother-of-pearl is a colour of great significance to Atlanteans with regard to healing, especially for problems of the bladder or womb.

Pink has its own unique place. It is rarely visible in the essence but is held clearly in the flower itself. It is a bringer of gentleness, calm and tranquillity, holding its own healing properties through these very virtues, literally putting one 'in the pink'. The term 'in the pink' must surely relate to those moments when there is complete attunement and harmony within the whole being, that time when loving oneself spiritually and mentally enables physical well-being to follow.

Feedback on the use of the pink 'Balance' oils containing the essences already mentioned has proved that they are of great benefit wherever there is over-activity in the growth of cells.

Orange and gold

Flowers, like people, have their own aura identity colour. As the flower colour often coincides with a human chakra colour, one has a definite lead into what is the plant's possible use in healing, on all three levels, physical, mental and spiritual. So we find the deep orange calendula (marigold) is closely connected to the 'gut reaction' on the memory plane, and deals with shocks, and karmas that stay over the centuries as well as those in the present that are creating blocks, fears and loss of energy. The deep golden marigold, allied in its very colour to the solar plexus area, the 'spaghetti junction' of the being, is a prophylactic, and also powerful for removing blocks originating in the past or the present that are allied to skin and nerve problems. It brings in the sunlight to unravel mind and muscle. By using Aura-Soma Calendula Beauty Bath, perfect balance, ease and renewal is achieved.

Into this chakra area are gathered all the lemon-scented plants – melissa (balm), the gentle one, lemon grass and citronella to name but three. All the citrics are valuable in combating alien forces and aggressive substances or situations. They provide their own sunlight and vitamin C, tossing their contribution into the bowl of healing, a veritable golden sheaf of life and light.

Shall we visualize next, the sprays of orange blossom worn

by and given to brides and those embarking on a new life. The essence of orange-blossom, known as neroli, has I believe a rather special association with the orange-growing countries. There are some who may well find that this particular essence, apart from its many other uses, can induce memories of previous incarnations in Mediterranean countries. The test of the essence is usually one's own resonance to it. Bear in mind that where there is a real aversion one might find that a painful experience occurred, either in the past or in the beginning of this earth life. It is well to use this essence for karmic clearance, as it is the block that brings the reaction.

How many times does a smell fling one back in time? The unexpected scent of a forgotten childhood association can suddenly stir up memories. There is a mystery about neroli, and it is interesting to note that the person who cannot relate to it is the one who has no wish to look back upon the past. Because of the association of neroli with the past and the present, and because dreams and the insomnia syndrome are usually associated with past memories or present problems, it is easy to understand why this essence, either one or two drops in the bath water, or in the form of orange-flower water, has a soporific effect. As a perfume it is most acceptable to some, and a drop placed behind the ear has brought astonishing reports of 'third eye' openings.

The golden sunflower, its face turned eternally to the sun, its heart exposing the very seed of its existence, takes its place with all the essences. The sunflower is in fact a catalyst for them all, a spiritual container, as it were, in which they may all lie in suspension as in the womb of Mother Earth.

We cannot walk away without a small backward glance at the sweet chamomile with her gentle fingers that smooth away all little upsets within the digestive tract. Her ability to touch the hair with sunshine, restoring and bringing forth the gold that lies within, is wondrous to behold.

Green

Now we reach the green, the heart chakra, the space-giver, the controller, the healer, the 'all in all', a true carrier of calm and eradicator of karma, the complementary colour of all the healing herbs and essences, for every plant has the green basis in its stems and leaves.

Once, a colour therapist commented on the blue and green 'Balance' combination, the exquisite jewel of the heart. 'You can't use blue and green together,' she said in horror.

'Why not?' I asked blankly, for all my combinations of oils are made under inspiration.

The colour therapist shook her head. 'They are adjacent colours on the wheel,' she said.

I smiled. 'What wheel? Had we not better get on the hot line to heaven and inform God that He has made a mistake, that the proud blue head of the cornflower resting upon its green stem, enfolded within its green leaves, or the sweet forget-me-not nestling in its bed of green are not in accordance with the wheel?'

There was silence. Not long after, the therapist was to change her mind, for the blue/green 'Balance' oil brought many favourable feedbacks.

It is apparent that the green of plants works in overall healing. It is the centralizer of the plant, the supplier and regenerator from which the whole being of the flower rises. If the stem is sick the flower suffers. Likewise, in the case of the human being, when the aura is sick, the rest of the body suffers. Green can be applied to any chakra area as a complementary support for the other colour desired or needed.

Now we turn to rosemary, the guardian of the garden, aromatic, the defender against all aggressive elements. Rosemary brings in the activity of the mind and memory. She is stimulating, factual, and with her purple flowers and green foliage is effective at both ends of the spectrum in bringing about the well-being of the human body. That is, she deals excellently with head problems as a hair stimulator, cleanser and invigorator, and she assists in the bowel and all invaders thereof. Thus Rosemary is a top-to-tail essence, and a good friend to all!

In this category too comes bergamot (the leafy part), the green goddess, the bringer of complete harmony, sweet in essence yet not cloying, binding all together. Bergamot is an adjunct to all, yet, because of her nature, is capable of retiring into the background. She is a gentle soul who gives to all the unconditional love that is so needed within the plant world and within the human soul.

Blue

We reach up now into the blue and see instances of the colour of the flower having a bearing on the chakra area of the same colour. Here we find the cornflower and the forget-me-not. By the very nature of their colour, they relate to the top human chakra, the throat and head, and are beneficial to any needs in those areas. Past memories pulsate through the forget-me-not, the soul longings that seek to find their expression, the yearnings that seize one unexpectedly when the soul reaches up and out and cries, 'Do you remember? What about me?'

Blue is the peace-bringer, the heavenly one, and a relevant point, I feel, is that green has the depth of blue within it. This is especially true of jade, the healing colour and jewel of the Chinese, and of turquoise, a colour between blue and green dealing with emotions and spiritual realization.

Magenta

Magenta is a combination of the violet and the red ends of the spectrum, the highest and most powerful wavelengths respectively. Magenta, formed from the dyestuff fuchsine and called magenta because of its discovery at about the time of the battle of Magenta in Italy in 1859, proved to be a very effective healing colour. Magenta paint has been used with success since its discovery, and I used it in my clinic for the treatment of athlete's foot, and other fungal and viral infections. Pharmaceutically, it was known then as Dr Castellani's paint but it is now referred to as Magenta paint. If one looks closely at the magenta, one sees that it offers the best of many worlds: the pink of gentleness and love, dealing with the fontanelles of the skull; violet, the bridge to healing; and the red of the earth, the grounding power. The magenta of digitalis, the foxglove, eases heart spasms.

Violet

For the very top chakra we must think of the nodding violet, the deep purple of pansy, and lavender with her noble dignity and healing fragrance bringing into balance that which is under stress.

Minor Miracles

Back in the war days, when I was working full-time in the pharmacy, which had acquired a reputation for personalized prescribing, a senior officer from the nearby Air Force camp, an old friend, came to see me.

'We have a problem at the camp,' he said, grinning. 'Every Friday there is a kit inspection. This entails various officers going into the mens' sleeping quarters.' The smile broadened. 'Can you imagine, Vicky, men all sleeping in the same quarters? Boarding school has nothing on it. Just standing at the entrance can be lethal, and that's at least six feet away from the nearest occupant!'

I smiled back. Here was a problem I understood – bromidrosis (perspiration and odour of the foot), abbreviated to 'POF'. In the profession of chiropody that I later took up, it was a common hazard. I feel that of all body odours, this particular one has its own special place – at least one hundred miles away from anyone else!

Always responsive to a need or challenge, I took it into meditation and thus it was that 'New Bliss', named after the hymn I had heard – 'New every morning is the bliss' – was conceived. It was immediately used and appreciated, and continued to be dispensed from my clinic, bringing relief and peace to many.

I should mention here that, with all my inspirations and preparations, there always appear to be several levels and aspects. Margaret, from some instinct which I must confess startled me, decided to use 'New Bliss' on haemorrhoids. Her first subject was a doctor's wife. It had already proved helpful on sweat rashes underneath breasts and on thighs, a far cry, perhaps, from feet, but in each instance where other preparations had failed it proved successful.

This particular preparation contains an essence that is used specifically against aggression and all situations where threat or disturbance exist. Insect bites, swollen ankles and sprains all seem to respond. I have always resisted the notion of 'cure alls' but nearly 50 years of feedback have taught me to think again. I am forced to acknowledge the amazing merits of a lotion that was intended for feet. 'New Bliss' was subsequently renamed 'Foothold', and is now called 'Carefree'.

All my 'children', conceived and born through meditation and inspiration, appear in some unaccountable way to have a distinct life, purpose and will of their own. I can only feel that it is the life surge of the essences and living energies which the Light itself, the Absolute, places within them.

I move on now to 'Beauty Bath', which originated 48 years ago and was then called 'Body Shampoo'. It is a soapless shampoo with exceptionally deep-cleansing qualities that are balanced perfectly with essential essences and herbs designed to replace naturally the oils of the body.

Over the years we have had feedback from many patients using 'Beauty Bath', and many will use nothing else. They tell of arthritis being controlled and, in one case, of a 12-year-old neck injury which had resulted in an immovable wry neck suddenly freeing itself and remaining free from then on. When I retired from the clinic, and with the miraculous coming of the Aura-Soma era, the gateway of the New Age, came the injunction to rename all that had gone before. 'Body Shampoo' became 'Beauty Bath'.

All these preparations appear to be incomprehensible within a materialistic framework and yet we should remind ourselves of the error in trying to explain the inexplicable.

There is a condition which does not appear to respond, other than temporarily, to conventional treatment. It takes the form of pruritis or even pustules around the reproductive organs. Feedback began to pour in. The condition seemed to respond to one particular chakra colour of the 'Beauty Bath', the primrose-coloured one with its special extracts and essences.

Purely as a preservative of youth and beauty, 'Beauty Bath' has more than proved its worth. When we were in Denmark during the Chernobyl fall-out, iodine tablets were immediately advocated through the media. Iodine, of course, is necessary for the thyroid which is vulnerable in radioactive conditions. This was soon countermanded when allergic reactions became evident. Mike had them. He substituted our Seaweed Mineral Bath which, when used in the bath, allows the iodine content to be absorbed at a rate which the body can assimilate. This was a valuable addition to the established use for water retention and detoxification.

Through unseen hands that have guided and conceived in some mysterious way, there is a transmutation within all these substances that pass through my hands to meet and greet the 're-new-all' needs of this rainbow age.

Many little miracles have been made, each seemingly designated for a specific purpose far beyond that first intended. All contain energies that would appear to reach back into timelessness, and are bound up with the most ancient of healing arts.

Sources of Healing

All aspects of God's creation – flower, forest, land, sea – can be sources of healing. Each of these living energies has its own purpose and power. The whole huge area of healing has many facets dispensed among those in attunement on all levels of understanding. Thus the green-fingered gardener plays his part, healing the earth, tending the plants, contributing his intuitive knowledge with an outpouring of creative love. The ancient apothecary well understood and used the alchemy of the plant world, harnessing and transmuting its live energies for the healing of the human and animal kingdoms.

Plants provide healing in various ways. Some by their sheer beauty, bring a promise of new life, new hope and a lifting of the spirit; some give of their eternal life, the essence of their being, for healing; some heal by the power of their colour vibrations in relation to the chakra wavelengths.

And then there are the clairvoyants and all those who see through the veil, for they are not hampered by the human concept of time. The past and the future are but 'timeslips'. Their gift, when used correctly, can be a source of holistic healing, dealing with the needs of the body, mind and spirit.

Often I find when the term healer is used the immediate assumption is of the laying on of hands. With many healers this is the case. I have witnessed a good number of such healings and felt the angels guiding the hands that have touched. There are many levels of healing, however.

The listening ear can bring release, a cleansing of frustrations, bitterness, apprehension or deep inner disturbances. It may not be spectacular or instantaneous healing, but the process has started. The need for love is universal. A greeting, a smile, a tender touch, each plays its part. The gateway to all healing is dedication, and the key that opens the gate is love.

Such trains of thought are now being studied and followed by the discerning, the New Age thinkers, who are aware of the importance of healing through the senses of vision, smell and hearing – colour, aroma and sound.

It is my firm belief that healing is ultimately Divine; anyone else involved in it is but a channel. Until the 'I' of self is crossed out, in other words unless the ego is sacrificed, the healer does not come into full power. The person must become a receiving vessel before he can perform his true function. With me, it has never been a conscious act – it is always an unconscious usage by the Higher Consciousness. It happens unsought, unbidden, and this is why I hesitate to say I am a healer, a clairvoyant or anything, because in the end I am nothing, and unless I remain nothing, precisely nothing will happen. Terms are merely man-made; those who heal work through the spirit and are known, but nameless.

I have already related the first healing episode that happened when I was about 11 years of age. Although I have always been reluctant to speak about them, I record here further incidents to which readers may relate. But I claim nothing – nothing but the ability to be used. That is all, and I do not think any healer can claim anything else. Healing is not an art, not something that can be gained by practice or technique. It is something that is given and can – and this is a word of warning – just as easily be taken away if it is not used correctly. If you abuse it, you lose it. I am sometimes asked: 'Can you teach me to heal?' How can I? We are talking of the Divine. It is not a conscious act or something that one can induce.

Why should there be a mediator? Even to turn on a wireless and receive a wave-length one needs to have a medium through which to do so. The word medium means exactly that – it is the means of attuning to the Divine wave-length for the healing.

I believe that any person who considers he needs healing should pray that the right channel will be sent, through which the Divine may work. Then in some weird and wonderful way a healer will be directed towards the right place at the right time.

The following incidents were all unsought and against my active will. The time was not sympathetic to such happenings. I could not and did not discuss them with anyone for fear of ridicule.

The healing I shall describe first took place when I was a struggling young practitioner in Great Missenden. The village contained a cross-section of society, ranging from earls to farm labourers. I was beginning to build up a rapport with those who came. They knew I cared.

One morning brought me Mrs X, a dear little soul who had been in service at a big house. As she sat down I noticed that the usual smile and cheerfulness were absent. I could feel her depression. I opened the conversation very carefully, giving her time to settle down.

'How are you, my dear?'

I glanced up momentarily. Yes, tears had started to form in her eyes.

'I'm very upset, Miss Wall', she said, and now the tears were really flowing. I stopped what I was doing but my hands remained upon her. I gave her all my attention.

'I've been to see the doctor about my eyes', she continued. 'He told me I have cataracts and will have to have an operation soon.' She swallowed nervously. 'I'm terrified of anything being done to my eyes. I don't think I can face it.'

The terror was real enough, for I felt the shaking of her body. She lived alone and there was no one to whom she could unburden her fears. My sympathy opened the floodgates of emotion, and the shared anxiety brought some comfort.

I picked up her stick when she was ready to leave and escorted her to the door. I noticed how much her condition had worsened. That night in my prayers and meditation I held her in the Divine healing stream. I saw her bathed in a beautiful blue light and there I left her. I continued to hold her in my prayers and each time the beautiful blue light would envelop her.

A month later, I spotted her name in my appointment book. The bell rang and there on the doorstep stood Mrs X. She was smiling, and without a stick.

'What do you think, Miss Wall?' she said excitedly. 'The doctor couldn't explain it, nor can I, but suddenly I was able to see and I do not need the operation!'

'Wonderful,' I said, smiling back, and in my heart there was a prayer of thankfulness.

The second case I shall relate concerns a Dutch woman who had come to the Amersham clinic for treatment of a long-standing back injury. After examining her, Margaret Cockbain called me into her consulting room on some pretext. Margaret was a completely dedicated cranial osteopath. Her work was her life, and her first concern was for the patient. She had a true humility that could and would seek another opinion if there were any disturbing doubts. She had come to realize, through various incidents, that she could trust my instinct if I had a chance to touch her patient. I would unerringly find the area of trouble. No interchange of words was necessary.

The woman was lying face down on the plinth. I placed my hand in a reassuring gesture on her back, at a point to which it seemed to be drawn. 'Sorry to intrude,' I said, 'but I am one of the practitioners here.'

My fingers immediately felt the customary tingle. It was a few seconds before I could move them with comfort, and then only after the tingling had ceased. I left the room to return to my own patient.

That evening Margaret told me: 'You did a wonderful job on that Dutch woman. She said her back was absolutely pain-free, and I had not manipulated it.'

It was, according to medical judgement, impossible to manipulate. Margaret continued: 'As she left, she asked me who came into the room and touched her back. She said that it felt as if it was on fire. Evidently she felt better immediately afterwards. I replied that it was the chiropodist, Miss Wall, who worked in the next room.'

Three years later, during a busy morning surgery, my telephone shrilled and the receptionist informed me that there was a lady outside wanting to see me urgently.

'Has she an appointment?' I asked, wondering if I was running behind schedule.

'No', replied the receptionist. 'But she says she has come all the way from Holland just to see you.'

Puzzled and intrigued, I suggested that the caller might wait until the lunch break. This, apparently, she agreed to with alacrity. It was well past one o'clock when I finished. Somewhat reluctantly I invited the visitor into my room, for I was now conscious of a lunch-time gap that needed filling – in short, I was ravenous. She entered, gazing at me intently.

'Now, how can I help you?' I asked.

'Are you Miss Wall?'

I nodded.

'She continued: 'You healed my back three years ago. I have no more pain until now when I have a car accident.'

Her English was not perfect but her request was very clear. 'Please, will you put your hand on my back again? That is all I ask.'

I thought to myself, good grief, what have I got myself into! All the professionalism within me reared and objected.

'You know, it's absolutely unethical for me to do what you ask. If I do, and it should become known, I stand in danger of being labelled a quack.'

She gazed at me, fighting back the tears. 'Couldn't you?' she pleaded. 'Please? I promise I will not tell anyone.'

At the age of 49, almost at the height of my professional career, I could foresee a never-ending queue of invalids stretching out the door, down the road and back to John O' Groats. I came out in a cold sweat. A whisper of this and everything I had worked for would crumble around my ears. I had never attempted healing on demand. But I could not find it in my heart to refuse. I prayed silently and suddenly there was a light before me, and around her streams of gold and violet flowed. I laid my hands upon her back and the vibrations began.

After I had declined her offer of money, and she had left, I gathered the last shreds of my integrity around me, consoling myself with the knowledge that I had acted not for self-glory or recompense but solely out of compassion. For all that, knowing human nature as I did, I sweated for the next few days, almost afraid to open the local papers for fear of discovering news of my action in print. Silently I vowed never again to expose myself to such a risk. It is sad to think that such was the climate of the day that one could be penalized merely for being the channel through which the Eternal Light could heal.

Finally, here is an instance of healing involving Margaret herself. She and I had just bidden a last farewell to a great friend, Sylvia, a brilliant young journalist who not so long ago had burst in with the news that she had received an inner injunction to work with herbs. Her life had been full of enthusiasm and expectancy; she was clearly 'on fire'. Sylvia had always used my creams, and had shown great interest in the flowers of the earth and their potencies. But suddenly a rare illness had overtaken her, and in spite of our agonized prayers, within a few short weeks she had departed on her onward journey. We were numbed with shock, as was her husband. Here was the finishing of a brilliant young life for no apparent reason. I was in the absolute depths of despondency and went into a 'dry' period spiritually.

It was in this downcast mood that Margaret and I decided to take a well-earned holiday on the Isle of Wight. A friend, a district nurse, was to join us for one or two days. I still had my sight at that time, and as I enjoyed motoring I undertook practically all of the driving in my ancient Wolseley, a beautiful vehicle built as solidly as a tank, and of which I was very proud.

Having collected our friend from the station, stowed her luggage in the boot and deposited her safely in the back seat, Margaret was about to sit next to me when the thought occurred to her that she might have left the boot open. How she managed it I will never know, but in leaning out of the open door to glance back, she placed her fingers within its hinges and in the same movement heartily slammed the door. Her hand was trapped, two fingers bent backwards. Our friend and I had literally to prize open the door to release them. Margaret turned as white as a sheet. The pain must have been intense.

'Oh God,' said the friend, 'let's go straight to the hospital, Vicky.'

I think I may humbly claim to be a sensitive, sympathetic character and normally would have felt panic at such a disaster. Margaret's precious hands! The hands that healed through her work perhaps now rendered useless by this terrible accident! But then the strangest thing happened. A calm came over me. Until then I had not uttered a word.

'Put your fingers in your mouth', I said quite casually. 'They'll be all right'

My mind and body seemingly had detached and suddenly I saw her hand as whole. Our friend in the back seat was breathing fire. I could feel her thoughts and her incredulity at what appeared to be my utter callousness. With conviction she repeated: 'Take her to the hospital immediately! It's an emergency'. Then, as I drove off, she exclaimed, 'Where are you going?'

'Home', I said quietly (home being the holiday caravan where we were staying). I drove up, and we looked at the fingers. There was nothing abnormal to be seen. Our friend said disbelievingly: 'It'll probably swell up tomorrow. I still think you should have it X-rayed today'

But the days came and went and the fingers functioned normally. There was no pain, discoloration, bruising or discomfort at all. Today, 20 years later, Margaret confirms that there is a complete absence of arthritis or damage in that hand. But with the passage of time her other hand shows signs of wear and tear, and understandably so, for her hands have been in constant use in her professional career.

The lesson I learned was rather important, for that day was a distinct step forward in the knowledge of healing. How many times have we agonized and prayed for a miracle of healing, only to find that a dear soul had slipped away, out of reach, and we wondered why? For we have cared so burningly, loved so deeply, prayed so tirelessly, and still the person had gone. It was at the moment described above that I was taught deliberate detachment, a moving out of the body into the astral state of being where earthbound emotions cannot intrude and one is in complete touch and linked to the Eternal Consciousness.

Many healers find it hard to heal within an intimate relationship, simply because it is almost impossible for them to detach. I have since tried to develop this ability of astral travel within personal situations, and found it does work. As with the body, so with the soul – there is no open sesame, for its progress is always one of stretching and growing.

Here is an interesting epilogue. After a lapse of about 15 years, when at one of our exhibitions, I was hailed by a voice.

'It is Vicky, isn't it?' The voice was hesitant.

I noted the aura – it was Sylvia's husband. No wonder he was a little surprised. When he had known me earlier, I had been a practitioner and 'Balance' had not been born. I turned. I looked into Sylvia's eyes. Almost as I received this, his voice continued: 'I am doing Sylvia's work. I am now a qualified herbalist.'

That he would be dedicated I had no doubt. My heart sang. 'Welcome back, Sylvia,' I breathed silently.

The Animal Kingdom

Aura-Soma ministers to the needs of the three kingdoms, animal, plant and human. Mystical, magical as it appears, neverthless it has an exciting practical purpose.

In the old days of dedication, it could be assumed that, apart from a few exceptions, those who chose to be doctors were already healers, and those who healed animals had an innate love of them together with a highly developed intuition. Nowadays, with materialism prevailing, ambition and professionalism tend to be regarded as sufficient motivation. But it is essential that the veterinary surgeon is prompted by an innate desire to help the animal kingdom as well as himself.

The 'Pomander', the beautiful blending of 49 herbal essences and extracts, is now being used by a highly qualified veterinary surgeon who has found it miraculously effective on animals, especially for ear conditions.

Eczema and various skin conditions in animals seem to respond amazingly well to the 'Balance' oils. It is also worthy of note that the chakras in humans and in animals have a direct correspondence. Our eyebrows need not lift at this, for are we not one in all? It is already well known that the pills, potions and injections administered by the veterinary surgeon are identical to many of those given by doctors to their patients, but, of course, in milder, adjusted doses. Therefore would it not be common sense to assume that maladjustments and disease in the animal kingdom could be treated on the same naturalistic basis as that of the human? Some vets are beginning to adopt homoeopathic treatments and New Age thinking.

There are groups which recommend the handling, fondling and holding of pets for therapeutic purposes. Heart and stroke patients have shown improvement after this 'treatment', and so too have people suffering from nervousness, depression and allied conditions.

Of great value in all healing, human or animal, is communication between healer and patient. Because of the lack of verbal communication between man and animal, the vet tends to be limited to diagnosis solely from manifest signs and symptoms. But the natural healer, whether he is a vet or not, guided by intuition, is able to have a silent communication with the animal, and so the problem can be discovered and treated.

The world is in sore need of animal healers. The harvest is plentiful, but labourers are few. I search every face and gaze at every aura that I might find those programmed for this purpose since time and timelessness were bound together within them, whether they are aware of it or not.

Horse sense

The following are actual excerpts from letters received from Aura-Soma therapists who, as you will read, had no knowledge of animal healing, nor were they practising as animal healers. It is worth noting that in both cases, and these are the ones we happen to have heard about, the same combinations of colours were used relating, as with all animals, to the human chakra needs. We refer to the all-orange 'Balance', the 'Humpty Dumpty' shock bottle, and the blue-over-purple oil, the 'Rescue', nature's own painkiller and emergency treatment.

'I was asked to see a valuable 12-year-old horse in the Yorkshire dales. He was severely lame in the rear near-side leg. I used the orange 'Balance' in his aura and was able with this to locate the cause of the problem – a band of 'shock' across his backside consistent with having been whipped or beaten many years previously. The aura repaired. I used the 'Rescue' bottle, massaged directly on to the pelvic, hip and stifle joints. After the first one-hour treatment, the horse was 90 per cent improved and continued to improve over the next three to four days. On day five a similar but much less severe problem occurred on the other side. (Having corrected the problem on one side, the muscular misuse of the other became apparent.) One further treatment was necessary, that is two altogether, and the horse was then better than the present owners had ever known. They subsequently told me that from his behaviour they had suspected he had been whipped or beaten by a stable boy when he was a very young horse.'

'A lady whom I was seeing for healing asked me if I could help her horse. The vet had diagnosed ring bone, a form of arthritis of the hoof. He had prescribed high doses of drugs, saying they would shorten the animal's life and that the horse would be on them for ever more.

'The lady was very worried and asked if I could give the animal healing. As it was not possible to visit, I said I would send absent healing. I suggested she use the orange Aura-Soma on the outside form of the animal as a "getting-together" after the use of drugs, to be followed by the "Rescue Remedy" on the hoof and bone. When the vet returned he was amazed at the improvement, stopped all drugs and said he had no answer to it. He also confirmed that the complaint was more in the bone I had spoken of. I don't remember speaking of the bone, but the lady assures me I did. I then felt the need to recommend the all-green bottle, which is now in use. The animal is looking and feeling very well.

'I should mention I know *nothing* about horses and do not feel "in tune" with them at all.'

There is a great field here to explore, a tremendous potential, and should we not make hay while the sun shines?

One episode of animal healing comes immediately to mind. It was many years ago, during the war, when I was living and working in West Drayton. At that time we were acquainted with a dog and cat breeder who used our pharmacy regularly. As the months passed, friendship grew.

Honour Bazeley and her husband, a sculptor of some renown, lived on a tiny island. The breeding kennels were secured by high wire fences, not only to protect and keep in their valuable pedigree dogs and cats but also to keep out animal or human intruders. The only entrance was through a high padlocked gate well protected against curious climbers or trepassers by a barbed-wire surround. It was a veritable Fort Knox. As it was so isolated and they were now quite elderly, entry was usually arranged by telephone appointment. I mention this point to emphasize the strangeness of the following episode, for undoubtedly there will be many who will try to find a logical explanation for the inexplicable.

Honour looked odd one morning – shaken might better describe her. Seeing this, I suggested a cup of tea in the dispensary. Tea was always readily available, for Miss Horsley was an inveterate tea drinker.

'Anything the matter, Honour?' I asked, once we were ensconced in the dispensary. She looked at me uncertainly.

'Well,' she said, 'I don't know if I've gone senile or whether it really happened, but if you'd like to hear about it . . .' Her voice trailed off, then: 'I must tell someone, if only to establish my sanity!'

I should mention here that Honour was, like most animal breeders, a very down-to-earth person, not given to wild fancies, and very much taken up with the material considerations of breeding as well as the pride involved. Her dogs were famous, and she exported a particular breed of Persian cat to America where it was much prized.

'One of my best dachshund bitches,' she said, 'has just had a litter of five. Four went immediately to feed, but the fifth was small and weak and the others crowded her out – most definitely a runt.'

Honour went on to explain that rearing her presented a problem, for the puppy appeared to have no desire to feed. The vet had called on his usual check-visit. Seeing the runt he said: 'That one's nearly dead. Why not let me put it down? Then the others can move more freely.'

'I refused,' Honour continued, 'just in case she had a chance, although personally I suspected he was right'.

The next day there was no improvement and if anything the little runt had grown weaker. The end was imminent.

'I picked it up out of the bed, really to prevent it being crushed by the others. It was hardly breathing. As I held it, I was suddenly aware of someone standing behind me. Strangely I did not feel alarmed or even disturbed, but still more strange was the uncanny silence'.

A normal approach of footsteps, even to the gate, would instantly set up a cacophony of barking from one hundred throats, as I knew well. Honour resumed her narrative: 'I turned towards him. I cannot remember any word being spoken, nor what he looked like or what he wore. There seemed to be no impression of a person. His hands were outstretched and without thinking I put the puppy into them. I was not conscious why I did. Still no words, still the silence all around. Then suddenly I found the little creature back in my arms. I bent down to replace it in the bed, and when I straightened up, there was no one there!'

Her eyes searched mine.

'I thought I'd better go in and have a brandy', she added after a pause. 'There was a feeling of something momentous, but what the heck it was I couldn't say'.

Later, when Honour went to feed the animals, she found to her astonishment that the runt was feeding as lustily as the others. When the vet next called, he said it was a pity that particular bitch had lost one of her puppies as she was a good mother.

'I told him only that the runt had survived. I didn't feel I could relate to him what had happened. I couldn't even tell my husband – I'm sure he'd have me certified!' Honour laughed at last, glancing at me to ascertain my reaction. I made no reply.

A further episode might be of interest, and again it happened in my developing days. I had become the proud possessor of three dogs – a German Shepherd, a yellow retriever, and Jasper, a dachshund from Honour's kennels whom she regarded as not good enough for showing or breeding purposes. Apart from their walks, the dogs exercised in the garden behind the pharmacy into which they would dash like three mad things the moment the door was opened, the two large dogs first, followed by Jasper, his short little legs tearing after them.

This particular summer, longing to create and grow, which was always my urge, I had planted one tomato plant against the sunny side of the fence. This plant was the joy of my life. I prayed over it, fed it and talked to it daily. I was young and it was the very first thing I had ever tried to grow. It flourished.

My eyes would go immediately to my precious plant the moment I opened the door for the dogs. Patsy and Judy would go straight to the other side of the garden, intent on their own affairs. Jasper, however, with a Pluto-like braking, would skid to a dramatic halt immediately in front of my precious plant, whence he would stop and watch intently. The first time this happened, his hackles were up but after that it seemed it was interest and watchfulness that kept him there, although his stumpy little tail would be kept erect, the sign of a dachshund on guard. I must confess that my first thought was that he would lift a gentlemanly leg against my prized plant, but I realized soon that there was no intent of that nature. His body remained quite still, alert and watchful.

I owned a small camera and, as any animal lover would, snapped shots of the three dogs from all angles.

The tomatoes, were now in full evidence – large, red, ripe and ready. I could not bring myself to remove them until I had photographed this beautiful sight. Our neighbour, a confectioner and newsagent, was called in to admire this wondrous plant and was promised the first fruit. An elderly lady, she was interested in everyone and had known the previous owners of the pharmacy.

The tomatoes were duly picked and distributed, and I waited for the return of my photographs from our develop-and-print man. On their arrival, I scanned the prints eagerly. Where was the one of the tomato plant? I found myself looking at our fence. Situated in the exact spot there was a vague indication of the tomato plant, but in front of it sat a black-and-white dog! In no way could this dog have anything to do with us, for none of my three dogs remotely resembled a black-and-white terrier. Nor could any other dog have entered our garden – the German Shepherd would have torn it to pieces. (I have shown this photograph to Ann, who writes with me, and there is no mistake. It is a dog.)

'What a nuisance, a double exposure', I said to myself crossly. 'Now I've lost the evidence of my beautiful plant.' However, protest as I might, an expert photographer declared that it was impossible for it to be anything but an actual photograph. It was inexplicable and annoying.

Later, our neighbour, having enjoyed the tomatoes, enquired: 'Did you get your photos back?'

I duly presented her with what to me was a minor tragedy. Instead of the sympathy I had expected there was a shocked look, and silence.

'Well', I queried, 'what do you make of that?'

'That's Nicky', she said quietly, 'the black-and-white terrier who belonged to Mr and Mrs X' (the previous owners of the pharmacy). 'He ran out into the road and got killed, about 15 years ago. They were heartbroken. They buried him by that fence.'

The photograph is still in my possession, almost 50 years later.

Here is another strange story about a dog and a lady known to me. Mrs B was making her customary journey by car to work. The morning was not a good one for it was raining, which added to Mrs B's gloom. Many dark stains had appeared on the patchwork of her life, all in quick succession. First there was the death of her husband, then the passing of a close friend, and finally the loss of her devoted dog. Preoccupied with her thoughts, she drove automatically but well.

Suddenly, straight ahead, a dog appeared from nowhere. For a second she could have sworn it was her old Rusty, the dog she had recently buried. Heart thumping, without time to reason, she rammed on the brakes. The next instant an approaching lorry skidded on the wet road surface, hit a lamp-post, and the side of the huge vehicle slid to an abrupt halt just inches away from the bonnet of her car.

Shocked and shaken, she got out of her car to meet the white-faced lorry driver. Before he could speak she said: 'I'm so sorry, but at least we both missed the dog.'

'What dog?' asked the lorry driver. 'Lucky for us that lamp-post was there, otherwise you'd have been a gonner.' He looked stunned. 'Blinking wet roads. I just went into a skid and couldn't pull out of it. No brakes, nothing. We were very lucky.'

She stared at him dumbly.

Driving home that evening, she went through the episode again in her mind. She had braked just before the lorry began its skid, and it was this that had saved her life. She had braked for the dog that wasn't there – or was it? Rusty, in his little heaven, smiled.

Animal intervention, and there are many incidents one could relate, is beyond dispute. The guardian angels are not confined entirely to the human heaven. As an animal lover, I have seen and heard of so many incidents that any other possibility becomes an impossibility.

Whenever a healing session is conducted, for me the inclusion of the animal kingdom is inevitable as the presence of animals is ever borne in mind. They play an important role in the protection and guidance of their earth loves, and evidence of this has been given time and time again. Their intervention, guidance and healing qualities are of inestimable value to us. (it is now a known scientific fact that the presence of a pet often aids recovery from serious illness.)

One of the questions I am asked most frequently is: 'Does Aura-Soma heal by faith?' Inevitably my reply is: 'I have faith, and God knows I have faith. But all I say is, does a horse have faith?' So is all this common sense, horse sense, or, 'non-sense'? The reader must judge for himself.

The Auric Flight

One day, late in 1939, the telephone rang and the excited voice of a friend greeted me.

'Vicky, good news!' The voice was almost singing with joy. 'Mum's home and the doctor says the operation was successful and that she will probably outlive all her children.' She laughed delightedly. Her mother was 70 and she herself 40. One of a large family, very close knit, she was devoted to the widowed mother who had had a struggle to bring them up.

'Come on over', she urged 'and drink to her continued health with us. We're all here.'

'Right', I said, 'I'll be straight round.'

Selecting the flowers took a little time. Instinctively I chose golden ones together with deep violet-blue irises. They snuggled into a bed of green lace-like fern and I asked that they be wrapped in magenta paper. It was many years later that I realized the meaning of my choice. I hastened to the house. The small bedroom seemed to be overflowing, the whole family had assembled. The strain of waiting during the long hours of the operation had disappeared from their faces. Their mother was home and apparently healed. A drink was put in my hand and we lifted our glasses in unison. Never a drinker, I put the glass to my lips and joined them. With beaming faces they gazed fondly down on their mother in the big white bed. They seemed unable to keep their hands away from her, an imaginary hair brushed back from her face, a non-existent crease smoothed from her immaculate counterpane, the already ample pillows plumped up – it was indeed a time of rejoicing.

I was standing at the foot of the bed, the only vacant place since she was completely surrounded by the circle of love. I smiled at her and she returned my smile a trifle wearily, under-standable with all the excitement around her. As her gaze wandered again towards her children, my eyes dropped to the hands lying above the sheets. Part of me suddenly detached, for there before me I saw her aura beginning to move slowly up and outwards to the left of her body. A golden glow had appeared on the periphery with muted blue above, while the aura left in the body had suddenly voided and paled to nothingness. Horror stricken, I watched this happening – I had seen it before. I looked away, telling myself that it was imagination. My gaze returned to her face, seeking reassurance. The face altered and I was looking into a death mask. Someone was speaking to me.

'Isn't she wonderful?' the voice said. The smile I tried to sustain froze on my face. I answered as well as I could and made my departure.

Early the next morning the telephone rang again. Brokenly the voice came over: 'I must let you know, Vicky, that dear Mother had a relapse during the night and we lost her.' The voice was choked, almost inarticulate. 'She was wonderful, wasn't she? She looked so well and happy. You thought so too, didn't you?'

I cannot remember exactly what I said, but I replaced the receiver and felt sorrow for the suffering of those left behind. The mother had been a saintly soul and I know now that the gold I was seeing was the sign of spiritual advancement, the halo of a life spent in sacrifice.

My first sighting of the 'auric flight' was with my childhood friend Cecilia, whom I visited when she was very ill. Of the seriousness of her illness I knew nothing. It was during one of these visits, shortly before she was recalled, that I noticed the change in her colours and their movement away from their normal position. It was something I saw while momentarily detached as in a dream, mistaken by some as day-dreaming. Something inside was hurting. In Cecilia's case the colours on the periphery were golden too, with the same blue coming in but with a diffusion of soft, gentle pink. I believe she was a gift to the angels, a message of love on earth. She died two days later, aged 13.

During wartime death was no stranger to anyone. Then, the auric sightings differed much. Many of those that I encountered were completely unknown to me. It was noticeable that shock situations and violent death had a different pattern. In the long, protracted passings one would see the true aural colours first before the 'flight' aural change began.

It was 1942. The worst had happened, a direct hit, and it was my first acquaintance with awful devastation. The bomb had struck an armaments factory. There were four hundred people in varying degrees of injury or shock, and so many violent deaths. With bodies everywhere, it was literally 'all hands on deck'. I was holding a young girl, trying to stop the hysteria that could have tempted her to run before medical personnel had ascertained whether or not she had sustained internal haemor-rhage or breakage of any sort. There was nothing one could do but wait for the ambulances; keep calm and wait amid the carnage. In self-protection, lest I too ran in panic, I detached, withdrawing my inner self away from my vulnerable body. It was then that I noticed a strange thing. The aura of the young girl had moved to the absolute periphery of her body. There was no golden glow but a fractured line ran through it and brown had appeared on the outer border, and there it stayed. When I saw her again a few days later, I noticed that her aura had remained on the periphery in its fractured state and had neither gone nor returned. This phenomenon was subsequently to be seen in many cases of shock, such as in car accidents, severe emotional situations and operations, and I have since described it as the aural separation or etheric gapping. This is literally the soul or divine spark going, as it were, into the 'slip-road' of life, which has been provided for such moments when the physical body has too much to bear, and the soul is trying to take flight until help arrives and healing can take place. I believe that the soul cannot leave its earthly abode until the allotted time, and is fairly held by the 'silver cord' that is never cut. Human hands can cut the umbilical cord but only the divine can sever the 'silver cord'.

I saw an ambulance driver take off his coat and place it gently over a horribly injured woman on the ground. Shock, sadness and horror showed on his face. Her clothes had been blown away by the blast from the bomb and she was exposed to the eyes of all. The heavy coat he had placed upon her had been an act to preserve her dignity. The respect of this act, in the midst of all the chaos, brought sudden tears to my eyes. The woman was obviously beyond physical help. Everything within me, for I was very young, wanted to run away, but it was my duty, as with everyone else who was able, to stay and help. My mind moved out. In this case, the woman's aura had begun its upward and outward journey. The golden glow was not there. The whole aura was shattered, pitted, the inner part almost black. As I watched, the blue began to appear and some gold touched the fringes, and I knew other hands were reaching out for her. Then, at that absolute moment, the face changed into utter peace, and there was a cascade of rainbow colours descending upon her. She was being recalled to her rest to be prepared for her return. This cascade of colours puzzled me, for I had not seen it before. The first time I was to experience something similar was when, almost over the brink after a huge coronary thrombosis which entailed resuscitation, I saw before me a beautiful garden, a cascade of rainbow colour with so many glorious hues normally unseen on earth. Subsequently, many in like circumstances, going to the brink and back, have spoken of a similar experience. I have been much reassured, for one sometimes doubts the reality of what one sees.

I have observed the auric flight in animals, too. Back in 1957, they had just told me, verifying what I had known for some time, that my beloved German Shepherd dog and faithful friend, Patsy, now 16 earth years old, had terminal cancer. The vet, a kind man, offered to help with her departure. I refused. Only the one who loved her and whom she loved would hold her, and there would be no pain in the outpouring of our mutual love. Nevertheless, I had prepared something that would help her through if the need arose.

The gaunt framework of her large body lay across me as I sat on the couch we had occupied so often before, the bones starkly visible. The large, now grey muzzle lay on my shoulder. I felt the familiar tickle of her side whiskers on my cheek. My hands cupped and cradled her dear face. The breathing became shallower and shallower. The time had come. There was a huge chasm of pain in my heart – we had been through this so many times before in so many lives and yet each time a little death had happened within me and the pain had never ceased to catch me unawares. My tears fell upon her head, silent, soul tears trickling down onto my hand beneath. Beloved friend, I love you so, I love you so.

Her beautiful, now golden aura began its travel. I watched the flight through the etheric body, and there was a light around everything. I watched her now in a haze of moving light and colour, watched her walk, as I had so many times before, towards the gateway and entrance to the evermore. We walked together in spirit to the very gate, a short distance, and I stood, for I could not go through with her. Vaguely I heard and saw the sounds of her friends greeting her and glimpsed the unseen colours and glory beyond as she entered. She did not look back. We both knew that there she would wait, as she had waited so many times before, for my return. With her, as with myself, we knew there would always be the chosen path of renunciation which we would inevitably always travel together.

The Vision

And I saw another mighty angel come down from heaven, clothed with a cloud: and a rainbow was upon his head, and his face was as it were the sun, and his feet as pillars of fire.

Rev. 10:1

It was now 1987. I was aware of the numerological significance of the year itself:

$$1+9+8+7 = 25$$
$$2+5 = 7$$

The mystical, magical number seven frequently occurs in prophecies and is said to be the number for the Rainbow Age, the 'Re-new-all' Age.

> *With light we come*
> *To this poor, tormented earth*
> *To bring a message*
> *A message of hope and delight.*
> *Freedom shall come*
> *As sure as spring follows winter*
> *Transformed, the earth shall beam in beauty*
> *And love and peace for ever rule.*

From The Flower Kingdom

The room was pulsating. Strange energies had been appearing for some time. I had a feeling of expectancy, urgency. During meditation, I began to experience movement within the room and a strange sense of levitation within myself, as if an invisible force were drawing me up. My whole being became involved. I was swept up into a new, higher dimension of combined powers which emanated from all the living elements in the room – the plants, even the wood of the chair where my hands rested seemed warm to the touch. Yet still I was piercingly aware of my earthly body that lay recumbent beneath.

As far as I knew, nothing had been altered within the room, the only addition being a deep purple/magenta-over-red 'Balance' oil which I had added to my little altar of 'Balance' jewels. It was here that I would meditate and obtain the peace and instruction needed for the day, re-energizing and regenerating physically as well as spiritually, balancing the chakras through the visual colours on the altar. There had been a sudden need within me, unaccountable yet unmistakable, for this special combination, the purple-over-red oil, which had been described as the link between heaven and earth. It stood now upon the little altar, glowing in its jewel-like beauty.

Something was happening. My eyes were drawn to the oils. Strange formations had appeared within all the combinations before me, symbols flashed from the depths of the oils (the mirrors), to explode at the very pinnacles. There were bubbles everywhere in excited conversation, moving, interweaving one with the other. The room seemed to be getting hotter and hotter. The feeling of being wrapped in a cocoon of timelessness enveloped me. There was an eruption within me, and I became part of time.

And in the vision, I saw the mountain move with a sudden upthrust towards the ultimate. The rocks trembled and heaved as a woman in travail. The very earth was opening. Apertures like mouths suddenly appeared everywhere. I stood in the midst of a colour explosion.

From the rocks came forth a brilliant flash of piercing amethyst, a huge laser-like beam of violet light, a ray cutting through and destroying the threatening blackness, the evil around, cleaving through and healing as it cleansed.

The amber sent its golden gleam, crossing the amethyst's path, pointing like a finger, revealing new directions, the wisdom of Solomon and the long-held secrets of the pyramids being shed upon the earth. A sharp shower of emerald light burst upon the scene, gleaming and sparkling, laying its healing light upon the earth in travail, spreading in gentle benediction, transmuting and transforming as it touched, its purity of purpose cleansing and creating a new space, a new polarity. From the burning ruby, glowing red with its inner fire, regenerating, re-enforcing with its earth energies, flashed flames that gave their potency in the fierce battle.

The deep hidden powers and energies of the earth were being unleashed. They crackled and resounded. The whole sky and earth were lit as if in a most spectacular firework display, a scintillating kaleidoscope of colour, and of interchanging shapes and symbols, each one knowing its own significance and purpose.

Silhouetted against the pinnacle of the mountain a figure appeared, dazzlingly, crystal clear, pure white light refracting the whole huge spectrum of colour in all its aspects. The radiance that emanated forth was blinding yet purifying. As I observed this glorious Being a sudden dark object, satanic in appearance, was hurled from the sky and plummetted down to the waiting earth to be swallowed up in the vortex of beams below.

The colour power of gems, the force of fossilized light kept in abeyance for just this time, had been released. This was not germ warfare, but gem warfare. Energies from all sources poured themselves out, joining in one gigantic force. Cosmic rays of colour joined forces in this final battle of light against darkness. The renewal of the earth had begun.

The earth lay now suffused with peace and harmony. Heavenly sapphire, sweet bringer of peace, communicator between heaven and earth, swept softly over all, touching and healing, bathing the world in the peace that passes all understanding. Peace for earth and good will towards all kingdoms.

'Dev Aura'

As the benefits of Aura-Soma therapy became more widely known, the demand for 'Balance' soared, and there were even more orders for the 'Pomander' and 'Quintessence' ranges. Our customers were from all parts of the world, in fact our overseas sales superseded those of the United Kingdom. Had money-making been our motive, this 'success story' could have become even greater. Time and again, I am asked if Aura-Soma can be bought in shops, and there is no doubt that there would be a market for it in shops and other outlets. However, we are not happy about people buying Aura-Soma without knowing what it is for or how to use it. So we make it a rule that retailers can only sell our products if they have had tuition in Aura-Soma therapy.

We do run a mail order service ourselves, and give out free information leaflets. But we prefer customers to have consulted a qualified Aura-Soma therapist before making purchases, except in the case of our 'Chakra Set' which may be used for specific ailments regardless of the personal aura colour.

By early 1986 it had become clear that our premises in Buckinghamshire were inadequate for our future requirements. We needed a proper centre where training could be given in Aura-Soma therapy, as well as sufficient space for production, mailing and general office work. How we came to find and acquire our Centre, 'Dev Aura', is an extraordinary story.

In the late summer of 1986, just after finishing an exhibition, tired, Mike Booth, his wife and I decided to have something to eat. Their children were with us too. As we went across the main road on the way to the restaurant, I turned to Mike and said, out of the blue: 'We shall have a centre within a year, and it shall be unencumbered.' By 'unencumbered' – one of my favourite words – I meant 'with no strings', we wouldn't owe anything. From the financial side there appeared to be no possibility as all that Aura-Soma earned was turned back for the furtherance of the vision.

An invitation had been received to conduct a seminar at a lovely manor house in Lincolnshire belonging to a member of our Aura-Soma family. Whilst there, on my usual morning walk with Mike I said, 'This is the area in which we will have our own centre.' Lincolnshire was a very long way from our home in Gold Hill. Such a move would entail leaving all London contacts and did not appear to be very practical.

Returning to Gold Hill, we were immediately swept into the routine pressures. Nearly a year later Mike tossed a letter on the table. 'This came through my door a few days ago, I meant to bring it.' Margaret read the letter. To our astonishment, as we had not applied, it contained details of a large Lincolnshire rectory with two acres of ground in the picturesque village of Tetford in the Wolds. Very exciting, as was the next bit of information: all bids had to be in by noon that very day! I asked Margaret to phone. She was told the property was derelict, vandalized and had been vacant for 10 years. Because it was Church property one of the stipulations was no mortgage. It all sounded impossible and improbable. Yet this letter arriving literally 'out of the blue' had to have a significance.

I went out to our roof garden and meditated. The answer came and I returned to the room. 'We shall have it,' I said. It was now eleven o'clock. 'How on earth are we to get them our bid on time?' asked Margaret. 'By heaven,' I said, laughing. 'Phone and ask them if they will accept a verbal bid if it's followed by an express letter.' They agreed. Now a further complication: what to offer? Again I sought guidance, and a figure flickered into my mind. We made the bid. To our delight (and slight consternation!) our bid was accepted. The old rectory was to be ours just a year after my prediction.

The rectory became ours in January 1987 and was renamed 'Dev Aura'. Such split-second timing in its acquisition seems to me to have been a God-given miracle. It is in a most beautiful spot, in the heart of Tennyson country. The vibrations there are unmistakably peace-giving and healing.

When I said the building was derelict when we bought it, that was an understatement. We had as yet not even viewed the property; it had been a matter of faith from beginning to end. On a foggy November day we went to view what was to be our Centre. The gate swung dismally on one hinge, the drive was a mixture of stones and weeds. A head-high tangle of nettles almost obscured the house. Broken windows peered at us, their frames rotting. Pigeons were roosting in the house, ceilings were down, pipes were frozen and obviously the electrics were unsafe. Despite all this we were elated. The vibrations were powerful yet peaceful and even in the midst of all the dereliction we could feel the promise of what was to come.

It took nine months of blood, sweat and tears, a truly Churchillian effort to prepare it for use. All the usual frustrations came about, along with broken promises and a hundred-and-one unforeseen snags. We would dash down whenever possible between ever-increasing Aura-Soma pressures. Mike became woodsman, hewing his way through the undergrowth and removing dead trees. In the midst of all this chaos we had the thrill of discovery, uncovering a beautiful old well which one day, when money permits, we shall restore. Also a coach-house and stable so smothered in ivy we didn't realize that underneath was a high south-facing brick wall with a chimney – perfect to use for a conservatory. We opened for our first residential seminar in October 1987. Today, two years later, there is a gracious drive and a lecture room adjacent to the stables, and the conservatory is now functional, providing our guests with organically-grown tomatoes, cucumbers and peppers, while the grape vines begin to find their way.

Dev Aura begins to show her true beauty and purpose, and has developed into an international academy. Margaret Cockbain lectures on anatomy and physiology, passing on her 40 years of experience as a cranial osteopath, and Mike Booth serves as my eyes and is my constant helper. We work closely together in spiritual unity. Mike will eventually take over and continue my work.

Readers, I have told you the Aura-Soma story and laid bare before you all that was within me, all that was secret. It remains to invite you on this exciting voyage of discovery and self-revelation. Do not stand by the waterside watching the ship go by when you have a first-class ticket in your pocket. Now is the time to be among the pioneers of this New Age with its new philosophy.

And so I come to the end of this book and cast off the stitches.

Appendix

Aura-Soma Balance Range

The key notes given below may be expanded through intuition and the information given in the chapter 'Subtleties of Aura-Soma 'Balance', wherein the first 30 subtleties are lovingly explored. Your interpretation will be an exercise in developing a fuller awareness of the many exciting facets in the wonderful world of colour.

0 Indigo/Purple-magenta	Bringing deep seeing and feeling into physical life
1 Blue/purple-magenta	'Rescue' – communication with the Being within
2 Blue/blue	Peaceful communication, nurturing feminine energy
3 Blue/green	Nurturing communication of the heart
4 Yellow/gold	Knowledge and wisdom, the thinker, the student, the teacher
5 Yellow/red	The wisdom to use the energies you have wisely
6 Red/red	The re-energizer and the basic energy for love
7 Yellow/green	The wisdom to trust the process of life
8 Yellow/blue	Wisdom through inner communication
9 Turquoise/green	The transcendental heart
10 Green/green	Space – 'go hug a tree'
11 Clear/pink	Clarity of mind to love the soul within
12 Clear/blue	Shining the light on nurturing, creativity and fruitfulness
13 Clear/green	Enlightenment of the heart
14 Clear/gold	Clarity of thought, New Age wisdom
15 Clear/violet	Elevation of the soul – purified healing
16 Violet/violet	Awakening to one's true self and service

17 Green/violet	A new beginning for spirituality
18 Yellow/violet	Spiritual teacher, having the wisdom to find the healing within
19 Red/purple	Regeneration – we renew our bodies when we renew our minds
20 Blue/pink	Intuitional love, communication of unconditional love
21 Green/pink	A new beginning for love
22 Yellow/pink	New perspective – re-birth
23 Rose pink/pink	Wisdom and understanding to find the love within
24 Violet/turquoise	The heart's communication of spirit
25 Purple/magenta	A pioneering spirit – a quest for spiritual knowledge
26 Orange/orange	Get-it-together-again. The shock absorber. Etheric Rescue
27 Red/green	Robin Hood – infectious enthusiasm for life
28 Green/red	Maid Marion – energy to find one's own space, pioneering
29 Red/blue	Right activity will lead to harmony and peace
30 Blue/red	Heaven on earth, life's quality
31 Green/gold	Knowing – through finding your own space
32 Blue/gold	A message of good things for the future
33 Royal blue/turquoise	'Inner-tuition' – communication of the heart
34 Pink/turquoise	Access to the hidden mysteries of life and love
35 Pink/violet	Service with unconditional love – love from above
36 Violet/pink	Kindness in service – compassion and understanding
37 Violet/blue	Nurturing and protecting – balanced communication
38 Violet/green	Discernment – balance of conscious and subconscious
39 Violet/gold	Knowledge and service to the whole world
40 Red/gold	Energy to find self-knowledge – expansive activity
41 Gold/gold	The cup runneth over – quintessence of wisdom on all levels
42 Yellow/yellow	Joy, wisdom, happiness, bliss awakening
43 Turquoise/turquoise	Communication of the heart – rely on your soul

44 Lilac/pale blue	Lilac flame of transmutation, blue of absolute protection
45 Turquoise/magenta	The need and the gift to have and to give love
46 Green/magenta	Discovery of inner strength and love
47 Indigo/lemon	Old soul – a time to formulate new goals
48 Violet/clear	Spiritual cleanser – a time to look within
49 Turquoise/violet	Elasticity of the mind through inner communication
50 Pale blue/pale blue	El Morya – the power behind the throne of consciousness
51 Pale yellow/pale yellow	Kuthumi – intellectual seeking and receiving of wisdom
52 Pale pink/pale pink	Lady Nada – spiritual growth through the ability to love unconditionally
53 Pale green/pale green	Hilarion – the pure heart, re-generation
54 Clear/clear	Serapis Bey – the power of the light, expansive consciousness
55 Clear/red	The Christ – light and inspiration enters the physical world
56 Pale violet/pale violet	St Germain – the walk along the pathways of the highest order
57 Pale pink/pale blue	Pallas Athena – 'let go and trust', personal independence
58 Pale blue/pale pink	Orion and Angelica – mother love/father love/spiritual love
59 Pale yellow/pale pink	Lady Portia – the potential for great joy and happiness
60 Pale blue/clear	Lao Tsu and Kwan Yin – be still and 'know' who you are
61 Pale pink/pale yellow	Sanat Kumara – the loving purpose of the Divine mind
62 Pale turquoise/pale turquoise	Maha Chohan – the sea of pure universal consciousness
63 Emerald green/pale green	Djwal Khul and Hilarion – new beginnings bring balance and justice
64 Green/clear	Djwal Khul – I am the way … listen and follow
65 Violet/red	The 'I am' comes to earth. Transformation
66 Pale violet/pale pink	Unconditional love in service of others
67 Magenta/magenta	Love Divine merged into service
68 Blue/violet	Peace and fulfilment, spiritual discernment
69 Magenta/clear	Purified desires, love's energetic drive

70 Yellow/clear	A vision of splendour
71 Pink/clear	Lift in consciousness through the limitless power of love
72 Blue/orange	Communication and nurturing of inner emotional desires
73 Gold/clear	Wisdom from the depth of the self
74 Pale yellow/pale green	Justice through balance
75 Magenta/turquoise	Go with the flow, a change of view
76 Pink/gold	Wisdom of the past expressed through unconditional love
77 Clear/magenta	Love and light manifest, physical perfection
78 Violet/purple-magenta	'Crown Rescue', peace-loving and dependable
79 Orange/violet	A deep healing from within for a shock situation
80 Red/pink	Energy to love and release. 'A letting go' bottle
81 Pink/pink	Unconditional love. Compassionate and understanding. The need for love
82 Green/orange	The space to connect with the insight from within. Deep bliss from the heart
83 Turquoise/gold	Heartfelt communications of the wisdom of the past
84 Pink/red	Compassion for the passion within. The desire to care
85 Turquoise/clear	New age communications. Inner illumination
86 Clear/turquoise	A channel for the creative communication of the heart. The light in media communications
87 Coral/coral	Love wisdom at all levels. Unrequited love
88 Green/blue	The communication from the depths of peace through one's feeling
89 Red/deep magenta	The Energy Rescue, the Time Shift

Enquiries about Aura-Soma products, courses, etc., are welcome. Please enclose s.a.e. with correspondence. Write to:

'Dev Aura',
Little London,
Tetford
Nr Horncastle,
Lincolnshire,
LN9 6QL

Telephone: Tetford (01507) 533781

The cover painting is available as a high quality art print (60x80 cm) and as a postcard.

For further information please contact the above address.

Index